IDEAS IN PROFILE
SMALL INTRODUCTIONS TO BIG TOPICS

D0259867
30130210330441

ALSO BY PAUL EDMONDSON

Twelfth Night: A Guide to the Text and its Theatrical Life
Shakespeare's Sonnets (co-authored with Stanley Wells)
A Year of Shakespeare: Re-Living the World Shakespeare
Festival (co-edited with Paul Prescott and Erin Sullivan)
Shakespeare Beyond Doubt: Evidence, Argument,
Controversy (co-edited with Stanley Wells)

SHAKESPEARE

PAUL EDMONDSON

P

PROFILE BOOKS

First published in Great Britain in 2015 by
PROFILE BOOKS LTD
3 Holford Yard
Bevin Way
London WC1X 9HD
www.profilebooks.com

COGNI+IVE

1 3 5 7 9 10 8 6 4 2

Designed by Jade Design
www.jadedesign.co.uk

Printed and bound in Italy by L.E.G.O. SpA–Lavis (TN)

ISBN 978 178125 3373
eISBN 978 178283 1037
Enhanced eBook ISBN 978 178283 1365

CONTENTS

For my godchildren:
Rowan Simpson
Eleanor Lofthouse
Harry Bate
Daisy Huish
and for
Freya Simpson
and
Sasha Hurley

A CHRONOLOGY OF SHAKESPEARE'S WORKS

This list (which includes collaborative works) is based on *The Oxford Shakespeare: The Complete Works*, edited by Stanley Wells and Gary Taylor with John Jowett and William Montgomery (Oxford: Clarendon Press, 2005). All quotations from Shakespeare are taken from this edition.

The Two Gentlemen of Verona (1589–90)
The Taming of the Shrew (1590–1)
The First Part of the Contention of the Two Famous Houses of York and Lancaster (*Henry VI Part Two*, 1590–1)
The True Tragedy of Richard Duke of York and the Good King Henry the Sixth (*Henry VI Part Three*, 1591)
The First Part of Henry the Sixth (1592)
The Most Lamentable Tragedy of Titus Andronicus (1592)
The Tragedy of King Richard III (1592–3)
Venus and Adonis (1592–3)
The Rape of Lucrece (1593–4)
The Reign of King Edward III (1594)
The Comedy of Errors (1594)
Love's Labour's Lost (1594–5)
Love's Labour's Won (1595–6): lost
The Tragedy of King Richard the Second (1595)

*The Most Excellent and Lamentable Tragedy of Romeo
and Juliet* (1595)
A Midsummer Night's Dream (1595)
The Life and Death of King John (1596)
*The Comical History of the Merchant of Venice, or
Otherwise Called the Jew of Venice* (1596–7)
The History of Henry the Fourth (1596–7)
The Merry Wives of Windsor (1597–8)
The Second Part of Henry the Fourth (1597–8)
Much Ado About Nothing (1598–9)
The Life of Henry the Fifth (1598–9)
The Tragedy of Julius Caesar (1599)
As You Like It (1599–1600)
The Tragedy of Hamlet (1600–1)
Twelfth Night, or What You Will (1601)
Troilus and Cressida (1602)
The Sonnets (1582–1609) and 'A Lover's Complaint' (1603–9)
The Book of Sir Thomas More (1603–4)
Measure for Measure (1603–4; adapted 1621)
The Tragedy of Othello, the Moor of Venice (1603–4)
The History of King Lear (1605–6): The Quarto Text
The Life of Timon of Athens (1606)
The Tragedy of Macbeth (1606; adapted 1616)
The Tragedy of Antony and Cleopatra (1606)
All's Well That Ends Well (1606–7)
Pericles, Prince of Tyre (1607)
The Tragedy of Coriolanus (1608)
The Winter's Tale (1609–10)

The Tragedy of King Lear (1610): The Folio Text
Cymbeline, King of Britain (1610–11)
The Tempest (1610–11)
Cardenio (1612–13): lost
All is True (*Henry VIII*, 1613)
The Two Noble Kinsmen (1613)

INTRODUCTION
THE SHAKESPEARE CURRENCY

A year before he died, a friend of mine gave me a Shake-speare sixpence. It has Queen Elizabeth I's profile on one side of it and the royal coat of arms on the other. Someone who badly needed my sixpence has bitten into one edge to check whether it was genuine. Certainly, its silver is airy thin. I call it a Shakespeare sixpence because it was minted in 1592, marking the time when Shakespeare was first mentioned in London. The Rialto Bridge in Venice was built that same year.

Shakespeare too was a coiner – of words. He was someone who freshly minted language, and for whom poetry, laughter, tears, intellectual stimulus and sheer entertainment were a *currency* that had to flow. He died young, about the same age as my friend, and left behind a body of work and a reputation which are second to none. In Shake-speare's time, sixpence would have bought me a place in the Lords' Room at The Globe Theatre to watch his company perform, or admitted me to their indoor playhouse, at the Blackfriars. As I hold this ordinary sixpence – smooth and bright with four centuries of touch – it makes me feel as though Shakespeare's own experience of the world is somehow within reach.

His words are a currency by which we can be trans-ported, too. The poet John Keats wrote a long and loving letter to his brother and sister-in-law, George and Georgiana, over the Christmas of 1818 and into the New Year. Like all of Keats's letters it is immediate and companionable, warm and affectionate and, like many of them, it includes thoughts and ideas about Shakespeare:

> Now, the reason why I do not feel at the present moment so far from you is that I remember your ways and manners and actions; I know your manner of thinking, your manner of feeling: I know what shape your joy and sorrow would take, I know the manner of your walking, standing, sauntering, sitting down, laughing, punning, and every action so truly that you seem near to me. You will remember me in the same manner – and the more when I tell you that I shall read a passage of Shakespeare every Sunday at ten o'clock – you read one at the same time and we shall be as near each other as blind bodies can be in the same room.[1]

For Keats, Shakespeare represented a currency of friendship, a heightened but familiar way of acknowledging mutual affection. But there is a deeper, spiritual communion at work in Keats's words, too. Shakespeare (any passage will do) is to be read at the same time, a Sunday at ten o'clock, and then they will feel as close together as it is possible to feel, though apart. Keats, incidentally, does not factor in the time difference: his brother and sister-in-law were living in North America.

Shakespeare has always inspired strong reactions, from extreme praise to sheer and utter boredom, and occasionally condemnation. This book is written from within my own reactions to Shakespeare, which have grown and developed over the twenty years I have lived, worked, written and taught in Stratford-upon-Avon. You never forget your first visit to this town. I was fifteen and was brought on a school trip from York to see John Caird's production of *A Midsummer Night's Dream* in 1989. The fairies were dressed as punk rockers and wore Doc Martens boots; the forest was a fantastical refuse site; the mechanicals' performance of the play within the play 'Pyramus and Thisbe' in act five seemed to have us rolling in the aisles. Two weeks later I returned and showed my mother and sister around the town, and we visited Shakespeare's Birthplace and Anne Hathaway's Cottage. We felt we owned Shakespeare, for a day.

This book is not primarily 'about' performance or criticism, though both relate closely to how I understand and enjoy Shakespeare. Nor will it tell you the stories of the plays (except a few, incidentally, in passing). But it will, I hope, explain what kind of writer Shakespeare is, where his work came from, why it matters, what he means to me and why I think he is worth spending time with (though there is never any moral obligation to like his work).

The first chapter presents something of what his life and career were like, the places he spent time in, some of the people he knew, and the world in which he lived. I do not subscribe to the cliché that everything we know about Shakespeare can be written on the back of a postcard. We know more about him than about many of his fellow writers. The problem is that we do not know what we would most like to know. There is no cache of personal papers, such as letters and diaries, but that is the case for most people of his time. Shakespearian biography often compensates for this lack of information by looking for his life in his works.

Here, I present an historical overview of facts about his life, avoiding where possible the stock Shakespearian biographical vocabulary of 'perhaps', 'might have', 'surely would have', 'almost certainly' and 'must have'. Chapter Two looks at his writing process, his reading and the life of the professional theatre, the shaping force of his imagination. Chapter Three considers *what* he wrote. He was a poet and a thinker who wrote innovative plays as well as a dramatist who wrote poetry. The fourth chapter seeks to convey something of his sheer *power* as a writer through looking at how he writes about love and sex, war, history, mortality, transgression and forgiveness. Chapter Five considers the primacy of performance as a way of encountering Shakespeare, the importance of theatre reviewing, and suggests how we might place ourselves as closely as possible to his language by reading a Shakespeare sonnet aloud to ourselves. The final chapter responds to the question 'Why Shakespeare?' by presenting a variety of Shakespearian cultural currencies such as performance, study, celebrations and political action. What is all the fuss actually about? Is he really deserving of his reputation?

1
WHAT WAS HIS LIFE LIKE?

If you wait outside Shakespeare's Birthplace on Henley Street in Stratford-upon-Avon for long enough two things are likely to happen. You will be in many photographs and you will meet someone from almost every country on earth. People go there to pay homage and to understand the world as William Shakespeare knew it.

The house looks large, tidy and respectable. Over time (and because of Victorian renovation) it has become an icon. Actually, the site comprises three houses in one, all of which Shakespeare inherited when he was thirty-seven years old on the death of his father in 1601. His sister, Joan Hart (whose husband died a week before Shakespeare) and her descendants continued to live in an adjoining property on the western side from the early 1600s until 1806. One of the first things Shakespeare did when he inherited the property was to lease it to Lewis Hiccox who extended it at the back and turned it into a pub, The Maidenhead, a thriving business which eventually made fifteen beds available to guests. Eager development of this kind puts Shakespeare squarely and unsentimentally on the side of moneymaking. Innovation and entrepreneurship characterised both his professional and his personal lives.

When Shakespeare's great-great-nephew, Shakespeare Hart, inherited the property at the beginning of the eighteenth century, the pub, later called The Swan and Maidenhead, moved to the eastern part of the site. Over the next half century, the main bedroom in the central section of the house came to be known as 'the Birthroom'. In 1759 Shakespeare's Birthplace was marked on Samuel Winter's map of Stratford-upon-Avon and ten years later the famous actor David Garrick spent a night there during his celebration of Shakespeare known as the Stratford Jubilee. He hung a banner out of the window. By the late eighteenth century part of the site was turned into a butcher's shop. 'Pilgrims', after having written their names on the wall of the increasingly popular shrine upstairs, could then enjoy a drink in The Swan and Maidenhead.

JOHN AND MARY SHAKESPEARE

William Shakespeare was the son of aspiring parents whose ancestral roots ran deep into the Warwickshire countryside. His father, John (before 1530–1601), came from what remains a small village, Snitterfield, about four miles to the north of Stratford-upon-Avon. Uncle Henry, his father's younger brother, remained farming in Snitterfield all his life and had various scrapes with the law.

John Shakespeare was more interested in self-improvement, but he, too, had his fair share of being caught out in a highly litigious culture. On 29 April 1552 he was fined for making a dungheap outside his home in Henley Street and in 1559 he and Master Clopton of New Place (the great house on Chapel Street which would later become

MARY & JOHN SHAKESPEARE

MARRIED IN 1557

INHERITED HER
FATHER'S
CONSIDERABLE
ESTATE

GLOVE MAKER
DEALT IN WOOL

SHAKESPEARE BORN 1564

William Shakespeare's family home) were fined 'for not keeping their gutters clean'. John managed to buy the eastern wing of the Henley Street home in 1556 and another house in nearby Greenhill Street. In 1557 he married Mary Arden of nearby Wilmcote. She was her father's favourite and the most able of his children. As the youngest of eight daughters (apparently from Arden's first wife) she had, unusually, inherited most of her father's considerable estate in 1556, two farmhouses and as much as a hundred acres of land. For John Shakespeare it was a socially aspiring marriage; for her part, Mary Arden found a husband full of promise and civic intention.

John served on the Town Council and was a tradesman, whose 'mystery' or craft was that of a 'whittawer', a worker with white leather, and a maker of gloves. John used the symbol of a pair of glover's compasses instead of a signature when witnessing an assessment of fines in 1559 and 1561, and again in 1564. He was of a generation that did not need to write (which does not mean he could not read). It is sometimes said that he would have prepared the leather he needed for his craft at the back of the birthplace, but this is doubtful. Leather making then, as now, was a smelly business that needed specialist equipment and lots of space, and Stratford-upon-Avon had designated tanneries. Importantly, he also dealt lucratively and extensively in wool (a booming business), partly collected from the skins used to make the gloves. In the nineteenth century the landlord of The Swan and Maidenhead described finding remnants of fleece-dealings and wool combing when the parlour floor was being relaid.

John occupied several major public offices. He became one of the town's ale-tasters (an important role in a significant industry), constable in 1558 and 1559, chamberlain from 1561 to 1563, alderman from 1565, and eventually bailiff (the equivalent of mayor) from 1 October 1568–69. He was elected as Chief Alderman and a Justice of the Peace in 1571, and also served as deputy bailiff.

In August 1569 he authorised, as bailiff, two playing companies to perform in Stratford-upon-Avon: the Queen's

Men, and the Earl of Worcester's Men, the first time that troupes of professional actors had come to the town. William Shakespeare was five and a half. Another event burned itself into the town's memory during that same year. John Shakespeare was legally obliged to oversee the white-washing of the vivid medieval wall paintings in the town's Guild Chapel. The state, in pursuit of religious uniformity, required that any suspiciously sensual aspects of Roman Catholicism such as images were covered over or removed. Protestant plainness claimed to be more holy, if far less visually stimulating.

THE WORLD INTO WHICH HE WAS BORN

Stratford-upon-Avon had, since 1196, been a market town with the right to hold an annual fair. By 1564 it was highly prosperous with around one thousand eight hundred inhabitants. Its central location between Wales, London and towns to the north, made it a crossroads of commerce and culture, but it was rural and leafy with many orchards and a thousand or more elm trees. The plague that struck the town in 1564 killed around two hundred inhabitants, including four children of the Green family who lived just three doors away from the Shakespeares. Baby Shakespeare was lucky to escape.

Birth certificates did not exist but the parish registers recorded baptisms. According to the Book of Common Prayer, babies had to be baptised on the next saint's day after their birth or on the following Sunday. St Mark's Day (the patron saint of Venice) was on 25 April, a day which Elizabethan superstition considered unlucky. Shakespeare was baptised in Holy Trinity Church on Wednesday, 26 April 1564, after morning or evening prayer, in the old Norman font which can still be seen there today. Traditionally, Shakespeare's birthday has been identified as the preceding Sunday, 23 April, St George's Day. The patron saint's day coincides with the birth of the national poet. For corroborative evidence that Shakespeare was born on 23 April we can look to his monument in the north chancel wall of Holy Trinity Church. This tells us he died on 23 April 1616 (the record of his burial was entered on 25 April) aged 53, which means the beginning of his fifty-third year, hence the understanding that he was born and died on the same date.

John and Mary's two previous children had died in infancy: Joan (1558) and Margaret (1562). William was the oldest of five subsequent children. His brother Gilbert was born in 1566 (d. 1612), another Joan in 1569 (d. 1646), Anne in 1571 (d. 1579), Richard in 1574 (d. 1613), and Edmund, who followed in his big brother's footsteps and became a 'player', an actor, in 1580 (d. 1607). That means that by the time Shakespeare was sixteen there were seven people living in the small family home, which by our modern standards allowed for little or no privacy, peace or quiet.

The conventional view of Shakespeare's background is that his father sought and won public approval, position and wealth in the first part of his career and then made some bad errors of judgement, with the result that from the middle of the 1570s he fell on hard times. He bought two more houses in 1572, and that same year he was caught illegally dealing in wool (the laws had tightened) and prosecuted for charging too much interest on a loan. He stopped attending council meetings from 1576 until 1586, when it was finally assumed he had lost interest. In 1578 he mortgaged his wife's inheritance, and in the 1580s sold land in Wilmcote, Snitterfield, Stratford-upon-Avon and the house he owned on Greenhill Street. John Shakespeare's financial misfortunes made his eldest son determined to acquire wealth and security.

That is the traditional interpretation. The revisionist view suggests that the wool dealing is actually how John Shakespeare made a significant amount of money, that his eldest son was helping him, and that his father's wool and other business concerns were the main reason why William Shakespeare went to London in the first place.[2] John's selling of property and land is interpreted as his wanting to invest the money elsewhere. By 1590 he owned the larger, western wing of the Henley Street house, which became part of the home he had kept all his life. John's will has not survived so we do not know how wealthy he was, but if there were money in the family this would help to explain how William Shakespeare could afford to co-found and buy shares in the new theatre company, the Lord Chamberlain's Men, in 1594, and purchase a great house, New Place, in 1597. The possibility that Shakespeare inherited money from his father would help to explain his considerable investments after his father died in 1601.

RELIGIOUS CRISES

William Shakespeare's was the first generation to be raised within an established, reformed and 'settled' religious environment. It was a time of spiritual turmoil. Depending on your point of view, Elizabeth I (1558–1603) either instigated a religious settlement or continued a religious revolution. Her father, Henry VIII (1509–1547), in seeking to divorce Katherine of Aragon, had denied papal authority and introduced religious reforms (1532–37) that led to the founding of a new state church, The Church of England. Elizabeth's half-brother, Edward VI (1537–1553), had continued and furthered these reforms. Then her half-sister, Mary, had taken the English church back to Roman Catholicism. Elizabeth urgently needed to settle the matter and anything she did was going to be controversial. Re-establishing a reformed church made her the automatic enemy of France and Spain and risked tipping the balance of power in Europe. Strictly speaking the Church of England was not founded as a Protestant church; it was and remains Catholic, but not *Roman* Catholic. The Act of Supremacy (1559), which made Elizabeth Supreme Governor of the Church of England, removed papal authority and brought in an oath of allegiance to the monarch. Her Act of Uniformity in religion (1559), the main legislation which properly founded the Church of England, only *just* got through parliament by a majority of three votes: twenty-one to eighteen (and none of the Bishops present voted for it). The Act made it compulsory for the whole nation to attend a state-church service every Sunday: you were fined for not attending church (an offence called recusancy) because not to do so raised the suspicion that you might be a practising Roman Catholic and potentially seditious.

Shakespeare was six years old when Pope Pius V excommunicated Elizabeth and called on all Roman Catholics to rebel against her, making her 'fair game' for any would-be Roman Catholic assassin. From 1571 Elizabeth responded with anti-Catholic laws which meant that being a Roman Catholic, promoting Roman Catholicism, or harbouring a Roman Catholic priest could be construed as treason, punishable by being hanged, drawn and quartered (thirty-nine Jesuit priests suffered this death-by-butchery from 1570–1603).

We can but guess at the psychological trauma experienced by a people who saw their church's images of Jesus, Mary, the saints, biblical stories, mythological animals, wild beasts, flora and fauna, being scratched out or whitewashed over, their religious effigies smashed, and some of their priests being torn apart before their eyes, but the memory of this turmoil is part of what helped to form the children of Shakespeare's generation.

Even as religious practices were being reformed, medieval stories and literature, bristling with a Roman Catholic sensibility, were enjoying a long shelf life. Many texts and authors from a century or so earlier were reprinted throughout Shakespeare's lifetime, making the medieval mind very much a part of the living present. While Shakespeare grew up with a sense of an older order having vanished, its legacy continued to influence what he read and heard. Images were disappearing from churches and more emphasis was being placed on the spoken word itself; at same time the professional theatre was developing rapidly and becoming popular. Performances fed a public desire for both spectacle and word, and they did not judge or condemn.

Shakespeare himself was raised and lived as a mainstream member of The Church of England. If we go seeking his spirituality (which to some extent is synonymous with a person's imagination) we find that it embraces the visual and sensual with a particularity of poetic expression. In *As You Like It*, the exiled Duke Senior

> Finds tongues in trees, books in the running brooks,
> Sermons in stones, and good in everything.

> (*As You Like It*, 2.1.15–17)

The frail, old, confused and heartbroken King Lear enters carrying the dead body of his favourite daughter, and says:

> Had I your tongues and eyes, I'd use them so
> That heaven's vault should crack.

> (*The Tragedy of King Lear*, 5.3.232–4)

In addressing the heavens, the desperate Princess Innogen says: 'if there be / Yet left in heaven as small a drop of pity / As a wren's eye, feared gods, a part of it!' (*Cymbeline*, 4.2.305–7). If clues about Shakespeare's spirituality can be gleaned from what he writes, then he seems equally open to God through the small and miniature as through the grand and the awe-inspiring. His lyrical descriptions of the natural world and powerful human emotions are the theatrical substitute for those vanishing medieval wall paintings in the churches.

LANGUAGE IS POWER

Importantly, Shakespeare was also inspired by the classical world, especially Latin literature. A new grammar school had opened in Stratford-upon-Avon in 1553 (though there had been a school there before), during the reign of Edward VI. It offered *all* the boys of the town a free education and John Shakespeare was able to give his eldest son every opportunity to receive the schooling he himself had missed. From around the age of five or six, William would have attended Petty School (for boys and girls), where he learnt his alphabet, the Ten Commandments and the Lord's Prayer. From around the age of seven or eight up to as late as sixteen, he could attend 'the King's new school', or Big School. Its records, like those of many schools of that time, do not survive, but we know about the curriculum.

The humanist education that Shakespeare experienced is one of the greatest cultural gifts that England has ever made available to its sons. Grammar schools were part of the government's machinery to ensure that, as worded in one charter, 'good literature and discipline might be diffused and propagated throughout all parts of our Kingdom, as wherein the best government and administration of affairs consists.' The boys were taught Latin rigorously six days a week throughout the whole year, going to school from 6 a.m. in summer and from 7 a.m. in winter until dusk (with Thursday and Saturday afternoons off). The few days of annual holiday observed only the major Christian festivals.

The grammar-school system recognised that language is power, and poetry, an inextricable part of a curriculum, was used to teach the pupils how to persuade and argue, how to succeed in politics. One of the reasons for the great flourishing of English literature from the 1590s was that two generations of writers had benefited from a grammar-school education.

Behind a good imagination and a well-formed mind there is often a great schoolteacher and encourager. Shakespeare's teachers were Simon Hunt, schoolmaster from 1571 to 1575 (possibly the same Hunt who left to become a Jesuit priest and who died in Rome in 1585) and Thomas Jenkins, schoolmaster from 1575 to 1579. Jenkins was from London and a graduate of St John's College, Oxford, where he was Fellow from 1566 to 1572 (during which time he had the lease on Chaucer's house in Woodstock). He was followed by John Cottom (1579–81), a Roman Catholic whose Jesuit brother was tortured on the rack and executed with the famous martyr Edmund Campion in 1582.

The boys were expected to speak Latin to each other even in the playground and at home. Greek was studied through the New Testament. Authors studied in their original Latin included playwrights, poets, philosophers and orators such as Terence, Virgil, Sallust, Palingenius, Mantuanus, Cicero, Susenbrotus, the Renaissance writer Erasmus, Quintilian, Horace and Juvenal. The Roman poet Ovid was Shakespeare's favourite writer and provided the source material for his two narrative poems, *Venus and Adonis* (1593) and *The Rape of Lucrece* (1594). Ovid's

Metamorphoses, made up of many poetic stories about the transformation of human beings and gods into other states, showed the young Shakespeare the vivid power of the imagination. On Shakespeare's stage, as in Ovid's poetry, a person's physical state reflects their inner, imaginative and moral experience, from Bottom's magical ass's head in *A Midsummer Night's Dream* to Gloucester's eyes, which are plucked out on stage in *King Lear*.

The syllabus was demanding but limited and did not, for example, include numeracy. Nevertheless, the boys who benefited from the grammar schools became part of the intellectual elite of their day. Shakespeare, like many of his contemporaries, was trained to be a lateral thinker with a keen eye for detail. He did not need to go to university in order to write and think as he did because his mind was already full of rhetorical sounds and shapes that he could put to expert use. Indeed, it is often said that the grammar-school curriculum was so rigorous that it made its pupils as proficient in classical languages and literature as a modern university graduate.

THE FUTURE CLOSES IN

By 1580, Shakespeare was probably helping out with the family business and informally teaching his family and neighbours; education was something to be respected and shared. Then, just two years later, came his girlfriend Anne Hathaway's (?1555–1623) unlooked for pregnancy.

Shakespeare was only eighteen and still underage. Between 1570 and 1630 the average age for men to marry in Stratford-upon-Avon was twenty-four. In that sixty-year period, and out of 106 cases, there were only three men who married under the age of twenty. Of those three men, Shakespeare was the youngest and the only one whose wife was already pregnant.[3] Anne was twenty-six and only by marriage could Shakespeare avoid social disgrace. The ceremony itself, quickly arranged, was enabled by a special licence from the Bishop of Worcester in November 1582. What this all meant, of course, was that Shakespeare's life choices and opportunities had, by the time he was eighteen and a half, drastically narrowed. Although Anne had brought with her six pounds, thirteen shillings and four pence as a marriage settlement from her father's will, the burden of supporting the family would nonetheless fall mainly on Shakespeare.

How could the young couple begin to make ends meet? If he had had any prospects as a professional apprentice in his father's leather-working and glove-making trade, these were now ruined (apprentices had to remain unmarried until their seven-year term was completed). Their first child, Susanna, was born about six months after their wedding. Twins followed in 1585, Hamnet and Judith, named after the Shakespeares' good friends Hamnet and Judith Sadler who lived on the corner of High Street and Sheep Street. If Mr and Mrs William Shakespeare *were* living in the Henley Street house with Shakespeare's parents and his four siblings in 1585, it would by then have been getting rather crowded.

LOST YEARS?

There is almost no documentary evidence for what Shakespeare was doing from 1585 to 1592, but 'lost' undocumented time is not unusual in the period. Description of these as the 'lost years' seems more indicative of biographical disappointment than of anything more meaningful. Some biographies send Shakespeare away to sea during this time, or have him training as a lawyer or a soldier. A brief account by the diarist John Aubrey (1626–1697) tells us that Shakespeare was for some years 'a school master in the country', which could, since Aubrey was writing in London, mean Stratford-upon-Avon itself. That one of the brightest boys in the school should help out with the teaching seems perfectly plausible. Nicholas Rowe published the first attempt at a life of Shakespeare at the front of his edition of the plays in 1709. He sent the actor Thomas Betterton to Stratford-upon-Avon to collect oral history from people who remembered Shakespeare and his family. Rowe reports that Shakespeare was caught and prosecuted for poaching deer from the estate of Sir Thomas Lucy at Charlecote (about five miles from Stratford-upon-Avon) and that he left (or escaped?) from

UNDERAGE MARRIAGE LICENCE

I DOTH

WILLIAM 18   ANNE 26

MARRIED ANNE HATHAWAY 1582

Warwickshire and went to London.

The deer-poaching story, although likely to be exaggerated, may not be as mythical as has been thought. Its earliest mention was in 1688 (within the life time of great-nephews and nieces) by Richard Davies, Chaplain of Corpus Christi College, Oxford, who also recorded that Sir Thomas Lucy 'oft [had Shakespeare] whipped and sometimes imprisoned and at last made him fly his native county to his great advancement'. Deer provided some of the skin that his father used in glove making. But perhaps Shakespeare first went to London after joining a travelling troupe of players such as The Queen's Men. Or perhaps poaching and play-acting combined to take him away from Stratford-upon-Avon. Or perhaps he was representing his father's business affairs. Whatever the reason, it was in London that he started to become established in what was to become his life's career.

3 CHILDREN
BY THE AGE OF 20

SHAKESPEARE THE FREELANCER

Shakespeare is first mentioned as a playwright in 1592 in *Greene's Groatsworth of Wit Bought with a Million of Repentance* by the popular writer Robert Greene (though Greene's authorship of the work is disputed). Shakespeare is resentfully referred to as a jack-of-all-trades, 'an upstart crow' and one who thinks himself 'the only Shake-scene in a country.' Greene then goes on to allude to a line from *Henry VI Part Three*, one of Shakespeare's early plays about the Wars of the Roses. Scholarship of the last thirty years has started to understand how some of Shakespeare's early plays, until 1594, might have been written in collaboration, a common practice for playwrights of the time. Whether on his own or in collaboration, Shakespeare had started to write successfully as a freelance and his was the name that caught Greene's jealous attention.

Shakespeare was twelve years old when the first major playhouse, The Theatre, opened in Shoreditch. By the time he arrived in London, professional theatres were becoming hugely popular. He was first associated with The Rose, the fifth purpose-built theatre in London and the first on Bankside, on the south bank of the River Thames. It had opened for business in 1587 and was the venue for some of Shakespeare's earliest work: *Henry VI Part One* and his bloodiest and most outrageous play, *Titus Andronicus*. The yard in front of its stage was big enough for about 740 people to stand and watch a show, and there was space for several hundred more in the galleries. It was there that Shakespeare began to be influenced by one of the most vivid and brilliant of his contemporaries, Christopher Marlowe, whose *Dr Faustus, The Jew of Malta*, and *Tamburlaine the Great* were also performed at The Rose.

The London theatre courted controversy with the Puritans who held sway in the City of London and with other anti-theatricalists who believed play-acting was amoral. The whole area of Bankside, which belonged to the Bishop of Winchester, was known as the Liberties and technically outside of the jurisdiction of the City. The playhouses stood cheek-by-jowl with brothels and sports arenas, spaces used as much for cockfighting and bear baiting as for revenge tragedies and pastoral comedies. If you stand facing the exhibition entrance of the modern-day Shakespeare's Globe and turn right you will see 'Cardinal Cap Alley' on the left. Although this sounds like a place where you might buy ecclesiastical headgear, it is actually named after a famous brothel, the Cardinal's Hat (which itself was named after the shape and colour of the top of a penis). Prostitutes of the Bankside were known as the Bishop of Winchester's geese (alluded to in the context of venereal disease in *Troilus and Cressida*, Additional Passages, B). But the theatre claimed social respectability. Each playing company needed an aristocratic patron. In theory, every theatre performance was a dress rehearsal for the time when that same play would be performed before the company's patron.

During outbreaks of plague the theatres closed to prevent the spread of infection. There were severe attacks in 1592–3 and, in 1603, the plague killed 38,000 Londoners (in a population of around 200,000). Outbreaks continued from 1604 to 1610. Whenever the theatres closed because of the plague, the companies usually went on tour. But they also closed for the six weeks of Lent, so there were plenty of opportunities in the working theatrical year for Shakespeare to make the three-day journey to Stratford-upon-Avon on horseback, to see his family, give them the money he was earning, and think about the next play in peace and quiet.

SHAKESPEARE'S BIG BREAKS

Shakespeare's name burst into print with his humorously erotic narrative poem, *Venus and Adonis*, dedicated to the nineteen-year-old Henry Wriothesley (1573–1624), the third Earl of Southampton. It was carefully printed by Shakespeare's Stratford-upon-Avon school friend, Richard Field, who had become a successful London publisher. *Venus and Adonis* was a sensation (it still can be to the first-time reader) and became the most printed, and therefore the most read, of all Shakespeare's works in his lifetime. There were ten editions by 1616. It was followed in 1594 by the deeply serious, equally erotic, and almost as popular *Lucrece* (which has come to be known as *The Rape of Lucrece*). Shakespeare dedicated this to the Earl, too, and this time in closely loving terms: 'the love I dedicate to your lordship is without end [...] what I have done is yours; what I have to do is yours, being part in all I have devoted yours.'

A story from the poet and playwright William Davenant (1606–1668), first published in Nicholas Rowe's biographical account of 1709, says that the Earl of Southampton gave Shakespeare £1,000 'to enable him to go through with a purchase which he heard he had a mind to.' Davenant himself liked to say he was Shakespeare's godson and illegitimate son. His parents owned the Crown Inn in Oxford, a likely place for Shakespeare to stay during his journeys from Stratford-upon-Avon to London. If Davenant was right, even though he may have exaggerated the actual sum of money, then a large gift from the Earl of Southampton would help to explain Shakespeare's spending in the mid-1590s. A useful comparative income to bear in mind is the Stratford-upon-Avon schoolmaster's salary: £20 a year.

In 1594 Shakespeare was one of seven (possibly eight) men to co-found a brand-new acting company, the Lord Chamberlain's Men. The Shakespeare scholar Andrew Gurr has reckoned that Shakespeare would have paid between £50 and £80 for his shares.[4] From 1594, he took up his role as a company man and their leading dramatist. That Christmas, Shakespeare is mentioned as having taken part in two royal performances before the Queen at her palace in Greenwich. An acting company was paid £10 for performing at court, which the Lord Chamberlain's Men regularly did, usually during the winter months and especially for the long Christmas season (thirty-three times before the Queen between 1594 and 1603).[5] It is difficult to be precise about how much playwrights were paid more generally, but even writing and performing in plays did not generate quite enough income to support a wife and family. It was because Shakespeare held shares in the new company that, from the age of thirty, he started to earn serious money.

Two years later his only son Hamnet died at the age of eleven. He was buried in Holy Trinity churchyard on 11 August 1596, while his father was probably away on tour. Referring to high infant mortality rates sometimes hides the pain of grief in statistics. To lose any infant is terrible. But Hamnet was eleven years old, and the death of a child can cast a long shadow. Two months later, on 20 October, Shakespeare's father was granted a coat of arms (there had been an earlier application after his time as bailiff). John Shakespeare became a gentleman, a status and title that

Shakespeare would inherit. But Shakespeare now had no direct male heir. In fact, after the death of his brother, Richard, in 1613, Shakespeare knew that his family name would die out.

During the years he was working in London, Shakespeare lodged at various places including (in order of residence) the parishes of St Giles Cripplegate, St Helen's Bishopgate, St Saviour's near the Clink, Southwark, and with the Mountjoy family on the corner of Monkswell and Silver Streets, again in the Cripplegate ward. Amid the headiness of theatrical life – audiences, box-office receipts, fellow playwrights, the next project, company tours – it was Stratford-upon-Avon that provided his domestic base. Significantly, he never owned a home in London. From 1597 he did not need to because he was able to buy the second largest house that Stratford-upon-Avon had to offer: New Place. He defaulted on paying his taxes twice in London while registered in the parish of St Helen's, Bishopgate (in 1597 and in 1598). It looks as if he left his lodgings in London at around that time while settling into his new Stratford-upon-Avon home.

New Place had been built in the 1480s by Hugh Clopton who had gone on to become the Lord Mayor of London. It was an impressive house with five gables and at least ten fireplaces, and was described by the Stratford Rent Roll of 1561 as a mansion house. Shakespeare had passed it every day on his way to school and it dominated the middle of the town, opposite the Guild's medieval chapel. There was plenty of space for Shakespeare's family and his move there was life-changing both personally and professionally. In February 1598, less than a year after taking possession, Shakespeare was listed with thirteen other neighbours in the Chapel Street ward for hoarding more malt at New Place than was permissible during a time of grain shortage. Malting was the town's main industry and needed for the common domestic practice of family beer brewing (since water was not usually safe to drink).

Only the site of New Place survives. The house that Shakespeare knew was substantially renovated by 1702 and then entirely demolished in 1759. Archaeology led by The Shakespeare Birthplace Trust from 2010 to 2015 confirmed the size of Shakespeare's Stratford-upon-Avon home, a tangible sense of the kind of status he achieved. There were extensive grounds at the back, some barns and an orchard with vines. He was continuing along the aspiring social trajectory he had learnt from his parents. One eyewitness account is revealing about Shakespeare's family life there. Rev. Joseph Greene (1712–1790), the headmaster of the grammar school, learnt the following about New Place from Hugh Clopton (a descendant of the original owner, born 1672) who recalled:

> several little epigrams on familiar subjects were found upon the glass of the house windows, some of which were written by Shakespeare, and many of them the product of his own children's brain: the tradition being, that he often in his times of pleasantry thus exercised his and their talents, and took great pleasure when he could trace in them some pretty display of that genius which God and Nature had blessed him with.

Shakespeare crafts words into the windows while his children watch his imagination unfold.

In October 1598, townsman, neighbour and friend, Richard Quiney (bailiff in 1602), was in London seeking parliamentary subsidy for relief after the devastating fires in Stratford-upon-Avon (in 1594 and 1595). We know where he was on Wednesday 25 October: The Bell Inn on Carter Lane, near St Paul's Cathedral. There he wrote to his 'Loving countryman', William Shakespeare, the only piece of Shakespearian correspondence that survives. Quiney asks Shakespeare to provide security for a loan of £30 to cover the debts he owes in London, while he, Quiney, is on his way to the court to fulfil his business on behalf of the town. The letter seems not to have been sent – perhaps Shakespeare saw Quiney before it was dispatched – because it was found among Quiney's own papers. What the letter confirms is that Quiney knew Shakespeare to be a man of means. Quiney's visit to the court was successful and the Queen granted relief to the town. Money was granted to help with the rebuilding, and Quiney's own expenses were reimbursed by the town council.

Shakespeare's means increased substantially in 1599 when he made another shrewd investment. Along with four other company men he spent £100 on shares in a new theatre, the biggest London had seen: the Globe. It was made from the recycled timbers of The Theatre, which had stood on a site for which the ground lease was about to expire. The wood was carried south across a frozen Thames and the Globe opened for business later in 1599. You could stand in the yard and watch a play for a penny or you could pay a few more pence and have a cushion, or sit in one of the galleries. Sixpence bought you a place in the Lords' Room (where you could be seen by the audience, even though your view of the actors was poor). The audience capacity in the new theatre was around three thousand and Shakespeare, as the company's leading dramatist, would make more money the more successful his plays became. But income fluctuated year on year and takings were always contingent on the plague. In a lucrative year, it is estimated that Shakespeare earned around £200 from his company shares and Globe receipts.[6]

FAME AND CONTROVERSY

The audience who crammed into the Globe to watch Shakespeare's plays were invited to share strong human emotions and political argument. State censorship was always on the lookout for anything seditious and all new plays had to gain the formal approval of the Master of the Revels, the state censor. Playwrights were thrown into jail and theatres closed if these laws were contravened. Around 1599 Shakespeare's printed works attracted the notice of William Scott who wrote a university dissertation called *The Model of Poesie*. Scott quotes directly from *The Rape of Lucrece* (criticising Shakespeare's tautology in line 935: 'to endless date of never-ending woes') and *Richard II*. In 1601 the Earl of Essex attempted a coup against Elizabeth with which Scott himself had some involvement. Essex's supporters employed the Lord Chamberlain's Men to perform *Richard II* on the night before the rebellion was due to take place. This is the play in which Shakespeare dramatises the deposition of the monarch (in act four, scene one), a scene so sensitive that it was not allowed to be printed until after Queen Elizabeth died ('I am Richard the second', she is reported to have said, 'know ye not that?'). Theatre, on that occasion, failed to ignite the audience into supporting a revolution. However good the performance, the revolt was a failure. But it was a dangerous episode in the life of the company, some of whom had to give evidence. Essex was tried for treason. Shakespeare's patron the Earl of Southampton was himself involved and imprisoned in the Tower (with his cat). Essex was beheaded; Southampton was set free early in the reign of James I (1603–25).

On James I's accession to the throne, the Lord Chamberlain's Men became the King's Men – Shakespeare and some of his colleagues were invited to take part in the coronation procession (there survives the receipt for the scarlet cloth they were granted for their royal liveries). A year later, for Christmas 1604, the Earl of Southampton asked the King's Men to perform *Love's Labour's Lost* in his house on The Strand. They had all survived the political scare of 1601 and, as far as Shakespeare was concerned, Southampton's patronage was now in its eleventh year. As the premier company of the day, the King's Men continued to perform regularly at the court (eighty-five times before the King between 1603 and 1616), with Shakespeare's plays regularly featuring in their repertoire.[7]

Some aspects of Shakespeare's life are controversial, including speculations about his sexuality. It is possible to interpret a gay sensibility from a close reading of some of the Sonnets, but the only surviving account about his personal life is found in the diary of John Manningham, a

THE LORD CHAMBERLAIN'S MEN

THEATRE GROUP CO-FOUNDED 1594

trainee lawyer at Middle Temple, for 13 March 1602:

> Upon a time when Burbage played Richard the Third there was a citizen grew so far in liking with him, that before she went from the play she appointed him to come that night unto her by the name of Richard the Third. Shakespeare,

overhearing their conclusion, went before, was entertained and at his game ere Burbage came. Then, message being brought that Richard the Third was at the door, Shakespeare caused return to be made that William the Conqueror was before Richard the Third.

The story has a once-upon-a-time feeling about it. Manningham seems to be recording table talk, but another version of it appeared in Thomas Wilkes's *A General View of the Stage* in 1759, long before Manningham's diaries were discovered and published in 1831. If Shakespeare did have any gay inclinations, he also had heterosexual ones, which appear to have led to at least one bout of marital infidelity.

SHAKESPEARE THE COMMUTER

On the whole, Shakespeare was able successfully to divide his time among his friends and family and business concerns across the two social worlds of Stratford-upon-Avon and London over about twenty years.

There are fewer references to Shakespeare in London after 1604, which suggests he was spending more time in Stratford-upon-Avon. He had many business affairs to attend to there. There were the one hundred and seven acres of land he had bought in 1602 for £320 (a significant investment which suggests he might have inherited money from his father), and in 1605 he spent £440 on a 50 per cent share in the annual tithes payable to the church, "'of corn, grain, blade, and hay" from Old Stratford, Welcombe, and Bishopton and in the "tithes of wool, lamb, and other small and privy tithes" from the parish of Stratford.' Together, these Stratford-upon-Avon investments yielded around £60 a year.

On 5 June 1607, his daughter Susanna (1583–1649) married the physician John Hall (1575–1635). They stayed in Stratford-upon-Avon where Hall had set up his practice. Their daughter Elizabeth was born nine months later. No other children followed and she was the only grandchild born during Shakespeare's lifetime. Hall was a solid and reliable figure, a Puritan pillar of the church and town. Some of his casebooks survive: the earliest record dates from 1611, but none of the entries relate to Shakespeare. The Halls would weather a social scandal when, in 1613, Susanna was obliged to sue John Lane, who had put about rumours that she had contracted venereal disease from an adulterous affair, for defamation of character. She won her case.

Shakespeare's mother died in 1608, the same year that the King's Men took over the running of the Blackfriars Theatre, an indoor playhouse which used to be part of a Dominican monastery. A group of investors was formed, as they had been for the founding of The Globe, and once again a successful business was established. Although fewer people could attend each performance the cheapest admission price was six times higher (sixpence) and the theatre could operate more easily during the winter months. The plays were lit by candles and there was more scope for special effects than in the Globe. As a venue it had a strong reputation for music, having been used for the previous eight years by a playing company made up of boys.

In May 1612, Shakespeare testified in a court case about a

disputed marriage settlement between Christopher Mount-joy (with whom Shakespeare used to lodge in Silver Street) and his son-in-law, Stephen Belott. Mountjoy had promised a dowry of £60 and in the end only £10 had been paid. Although the events under question had occurred ten years before, Shakespeare had to give evidence and admitted to acting as a go-between for the Mountjoy daughter, Mary, and Belott. Could Shakespeare recall the sum involved? No, he could not. His memory on this occasion failed him, but this legal case is the only record we have of words that Shakespeare actually spoke.

In March 1613 he bought a gatehouse at Blackfriars for £140, the only property he ever owned in London and one that looks more like a financial arrangement with other members of the theatre company than anywhere he intended to live. In fact, he leased it to a Stratford-upon-Avon neighbour called John Robinson, who would, three years later, be one of the witnesses to his will.

In 1613, Shakespeare collaborated with Richard Burbage on an *impresa*, an allegorical, heraldic-like device, painted on a shield with a motto, for Francis Manners, the sixth Earl of Rutland to use during the tilting to mark the tenth anniversary of King James I's accession (24 March). Neither Shakespeare's words nor Burbage's design survives. Both men were paid forty-four shillings in gold.

Disaster struck later that year on 29 June when fire broke out at the Globe during a performance of *All is True* (*Henry VIII*). Sir Henry Wotton was there and wrote to his nephew about it: 'nothing did perish but wood and straw and a few forsaken cloaks; only one man had his breeches set on fire, that would perhaps have broiled him if he had not by the benefit of a provident wit put it out with bottle ale.' A ballad produced shortly afterwards describes the event and includes the refrain 'O sorrow, pitiful sorrow, / And yet all this is true' (echoing the original name of Shakespeare's play). The theatre was rebuilt and ready for business by a year and a day later. But Shakespeare's shares in The Globe are not mentioned in his will, which suggests he sold them. The fire could have broken his spirit, especially if any manuscripts had been lost in the blaze. Shortly after the new Globe had opened, a major fire swept through Stratford-upon-Avon on 9 July 1614, destroying fifty-four houses, as well as outbuildings, though Shakespeare and his family were not directly affected.

There is a long-established (and lazy) assumption in Shakespearian biography that Shakespeare disappears to London soon after his marriage, is away from Stratford-upon-Avon for nearly twenty years and then 'retires' back to the town. But the notion of 'retirement' is anachronistic and suggests that Shakespeare thought he was getting old and was ready to leave the world of the theatre. Not a bit of it. Fifty-two was no great age then, any more than it is now. Similarly, his collaborative work with John Fletcher during what is sometimes referred to as 'the end of Shakespeare's career' is misleadingly interpreted as Shakespeare somehow signalling his withdrawal from professional playwriting. The two men worked on three plays together: *All is True* (*Henry VIII*), the lost play *Cardenio* (based on Cervantes' *Don Quixote*) and *The Two Noble Kinsmen*. This last is as innovative as anything that Shakespeare ever produced. The scenes he wrote are characterised by their difficult language, imagery and strangeness of style. On Shakespeare's part *The Two Noble Kinsmen* represents another new departure in a career that was full of innovations. Any work he produced after 1613 seems not to have survived, and who knows what he would have gone on to write had he lived longer?

LAST THINGS

In what was to be the last year and a half of his life, Shakespeare was involved in a local issue that would have affected the land he owned on the Welcombe hills and in Old Stratford, and the income he derived from it. There was a serious proposal to enclose a large area of open meadow that almost came to pass. Had it done so, the fields on which the townsfolk grew their crops would have become no more than pasture for sheep. Along with his cousin, Thomas Greene, Shakespeare took precautions to ensure that this source of income would be safe, whatever the outcome.

Shakespeare drafted his will in January 1616 and made revisions on the Feast of the Annunciation, or Lady Day, 25 March 1616. It survives only in draft form and bears three feeble-looking signatures, which has led to the conjecture that he was suffering from a stroke. We do not know what he died of but typhus has been reasonably suggested. An anecdote recorded in 1662 by John Ward, the vicar of Stratford-upon-Avon, says that Shakespeare caught a fever from drinking too hard while out on a 'merry meeting' with Ben Jonson and Michael Drayton (a poet closely associated with Clifford Chambers, about a mile from Stratford-upon-Avon).

He was buried in Holy Trinity Church, Stratford-upon-Avon, on 25 April 1616. The vicar who presided over his funeral was John Rogers, who was his next-door neighbour in 1611, from the old priest's house close to the Guild Chapel. A gravestone without a name on it, but always assumed to be Shakespeare's, marks the spot near the high altar with an epitaph of two rhyming couplets. They arrest the passer-by with a blessing and a curse:

> Good friend, for Jesus' sake forbear
> To dig the dust enclosèd here.
> Blessed be the man that spares these stones,
> And cursed be he that moves my bones.

A Dutch sculptor, Geerhart Janssen, made Shakespeare's bust in the monument on the wall above his grave. He had made the tomb and effigy for Shakespeare's friend John Coombe (buried near the high altar in July 1614). Janssen's father's workshop was in Southwark near The Globe Theatre so the chances are that both father and son knew what Shakespeare looked like. The Latin words on Shakespeare's monument compare him to classical figures and call him 'a Nestor in counsel, a Socrates in mind, and a Virgil in art.' There then follows an inscription in English:

> Stay Passenger, why goest thou by so fast?
> Read if thou canst, whom envious Death hath placed
> Within this monument Shakespeare: with whom
> Quick nature died: whose name doth deck this tomb

Far more than cost: sith [since] all that he hath writ
Leaves living art, but page to serve his wit.

Shakespeare, says this inscription, is a poet of nature, a writer of plays ('living art') and published works. The printed pages, like a pageboy, serve his intelligence. The effigy of Shakespeare is crudely executed but gives us some sense of what he looked like: high, rounded cheeks, small, sunken eyes, a high forehead and balding, auburn hair. He is wearing the scarlet livery tunic of the King's Men, harking back to the coronation of 1603. We do not know when the monument was installed but it seems to be a tribute from friends, colleagues and townspeople. Stratford-upon-Avon historian Mairi Macdonald points out that Thomas Wilson, a vicar with Puritan leanings, took over the running of the church in 1619 and that the colourful memorial is unlikely to have agreed with his taste.[8] The bust is likely, therefore, to have been installed by 1619 and was certainly in place by 1623 when it was referred to in the preliminary matter to the edition of Shakespeare's collected plays.

Shakespeare's bequests show that he died a wealthy man. The sums of money mentioned in his will, amounting to around £360, exceed those of many of his theatrical contemporaries, and in addition he owned land, property and shares. Susanna inherited the most, including New Place. The fact that Shakespeare leaves his widow, Anne, his 'second-best bed with the furniture' has raised questions about the state of the marriage. But the 'second-best bed' may have been the marriage bed, the best bed being reserved for guests. The degree to which the bequest is understood to represent a romantic souvenir or a put-down is open to interpretation. Certainly it is unusual that Anne was not named executrix. That duty fell to daughter and son-in-law, Susanna and John Hall.

Judith inherited £100 as a marriage settlement, interest on £150 as long as she remained married, and a 'broad silver-gilt bowl'. This bequest was no doubt influenced by her being involved in something of a scandal in the last couple of months of Shakespeare's life. On 10 February 1616 she married Thomas Quiney, who, like Shakespeare himself, had begotten a child outside wedlock. But in Quiney's case, the poor woman, Margaret Wheeler, died in childbirth, as did her baby. The day after Shakespeare had signed his will, Quiney appeared before the court and pleaded guilty to fornication.

The only grandchild Shakespeare knew, Elizabeth Hall (1608–1670), inherited the rest of his 'plate' (gold and silver ware). William Walker, his young godson, received twenty shillings in gold; Thomas Coombe (John's brother) had Shakespeare's sword (an intimate bequest which signals a close friendship) and his fellow actors Richard Burbage, John Heminges (1566–1630) and Henry Condell (1576–1627) were among others to be given money to buy mourning rings, a common practice. The Shakespeare scholar Stanley Wells has suggested that these bequests also signalled an agreement that they would publish a posthumous collection of his work.[9] Burbage died in 1619, but the other two men worked hard to publish an almost complete edition of Shakespeare's plays, which appeared in 1623. It is known as the First Folio (because of the size of paper it is printed on),

ALAS, POOR SHAKEY

HAPPY BIRTHDAY

GOOD FRIEND FOR JESUS SAKE FORBEARE,
TO DIGG THE DUST ENCLOASED HEARE.
BLESE BE YE MAN YT SPARES THES STONES,
AND CURST BE HE YT MOVES MY BONES.

SHAKESPEARE SHUFFLES OFF THIS MORTAL COIL 1616

contains 36 plays (half of which appeared there for the first time), and is Shakespeare's greatest legacy of all. His fellow playwright, poet, friend and rival, Ben Jonson (1572–1637), wrote a fine and famous tribute for the Folio. He refers to Shakespeare as 'soul of the age! / The applause, delight and wonder of our stage!' Later, Jonson would write: 'I loved

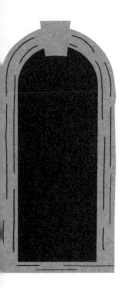

the man, and do honour his memory on this side idolatry as much as any. He was, indeed, honest, and of an open and free nature; had an excellent fancy, brave notions, and gentle expressions, wherein he flowed with that facility that sometime it was necessary he should be stopped' (published posthumously in *Timber, or Discoveries Made Upon Men and Matter*, 1640).

Anne Shakespeare died in 1623 and is buried next to the wall, beneath her husband's monument. Son-in-law John Hall died in 1635, and his widow, Susanna, died in 1649. She is buried near her father and husband. Her epitaph commemorates her as being 'witty above her sex' and says that 'something of Shakespeare was in that'. Shakespeare's daughter Judith had three sons, all of whom died young: Shakespeare (1616–1617), Richard (1618–1639) and Thomas (1620–1639). There were no more direct Shakespeare descendants.

In 1661 the vicar of Stratford-upon-Avon, Rev. John Ward, made a note to himself that he must visit Judith Quiney (then aged seventy-six) to talk to her about her father. Judith died shortly afterwards. One can only begin to imagine the difference Ward's notes from a conversation with the poet's daughter might have made to our understanding of Shakespeare. Either Ward never got round to making a record of it, or it remains the most important literary conversation of all time that never took place.

The earliest reference to anyone noticing Shakespeare's grave is 1634 when a Lieutenant Hammond, during a tour of twenty-six counties, records 'a neat monument of that famous English poet, Mr William Shakespeare; who was born there.' Two centuries later the novelist Walter Scott would stand on the same spot and, looking upon Shakespeare's grave, call it 'the tomb of the mighty wizard.' But how did that wizard make his magic?

2
HOW DID HE WRITE?

Towards the back of the inner courtyard of New Place stood the inner dwelling, the family home. Richard Grimmitt (born 1683), who used to play there with his friend Edward Clopton when they were children, remembers entering a side door on Chapel Lane from which 'they crossed a small kind of green court before they entered the house which was bearing to the left and fronted with brick, with plain windows consisting of common panes of glass set in lead.' It was a writer's house, and writers need books. Imagine then, for a moment, peering through one of those leaded windows into Shakespeare's library. In my mind's eye I see a book-lined room with a desk at one end in front of a south-facing window. There's a small chest to one side in which to transport some of the most frequently used volumes to and from his lodgings in London. But which books did Shakespeare need in order to write the plays? However we imagine Shakespeare's library, it is subject to change as our understanding about *how* he wrote continues to deepen.[10]

SHAKESPEARE'S ORIGINALITY

Shakespeare's contemporaries compared him to classical writers and when John Manningham saw a performance of

HOW DID HE WRITE?

ABSORB RHETORICAL FIGURES

ONOMATOPOEIA
PERSONIFICATION
METAPHOR

STEEPED IN THE BIBLE &
MEDIEVAL LITERATURE

INDENTIFIABLE SOURCE
MATERIAL HE USED IN

ENGLISH
LATIN
FRENCH
ITALIAN

TRANSLATIONS FROM
GREEK & PORTUGUESE

ACCESS TO
A LARGE
RANGE OF
BOOKS

THE HOLY BIBLE
THE CANTERBURY TALES
PLUTARCH'S HISTORIES
G. GASCOIGNE SUPPOSES
JORGE DE MONTEMAYOR DIANA
PLAUTUS AMPHITRYON

HE WOULD READ CHALLENGINGLY
AND WITH A STRONG MEMORY

CHRISTOPHER MARLOWE
INFLUENCED SHAKESPEARE'S
POETIC IMAGINATION

JOHN LYLY
INFLUENCED SHAKESPEARE
WITH HIS DRAMATIC PROSE

OCCASIONALLY HE WOULD
Collaborate

Twelfth Night, or What You Will at the Middle Temple on 2 February 1602, it reminded him of the Roman comedy *Menaechmi* by Plautus, as well as of a much more recent Italian play, *Gl'Inganni* (that refers to *The Mistakes* by Nicolò Secchi, first published in Florence in 1562). Manningham mixed up his sources. *Twelfth Night* much more closely resembles another work with a similar name, *Gl'Ingannati* (that is, the anonymous *The Deceived*, first published in Siena in 1537 and widely translated across Europe by the time Shakespeare was writing). Manningham's account reveals how Shakespeare was understood to be a literary writer, one who used different kinds of source material from different periods.

All writers draw from their own experience, too, some more than others, but where do Shakespeare's reading and imagination end and his life experience begin? The personality of Shakespeare's contemporary, John Donne (1572–1631), the poet, lover, philosopher, priest and preacher, is writ large in his work. It would seem strange not to read it biographically, at least in part. Shakespeare's writing was rooted in classical and humanist learning. At school he was taught to write, as it were, within literature, imitating the Latin authors. In asking *how* Shakespeare wrote we might turn the question around and ask ourselves: if we wanted to write like Shakespeare, what would we have to do?

HOW TO WRITE LIKE SHAKESPEARE

If we want to catch something of Shakespeare's tone of voice, then we need to become acquainted with the rhetorical figures he knew intimately. Figures of speech (and this is only one area of rhetoric: others include logic, memory, elocution and bodily gesture) are no less than the fibres that make up Shakespeare's poetry. Sometimes he calls attention to the rhetorical display of a character for comic effect. In the speech that follows, I have inserted the names of the rhetorical figures used by the fiery Hotspur:

HOTSPUR
By heaven, methinks it were an easy leap (*assonance*)
To pluck (*onomatopoeia*) bright honour from the pale-faced moon (*personification, adynaton*),
Or (*antithesis*) dive into the bottom of the deep (*alliteration, metaphor*),
Where fathom-line could never touch the ground (*hyperbole*),
And pluck (*repetition*) up drownèd honour by the locks (*synecdoche*),
So (*antithesis*) he that doth redeem her (*personification*) thence might wear (*metaphor*),
Without corrival, all her dignities (*merism*).
But out upon this half-faced fellowship (*alliteration*)!
WORCESTER (*to Northumberland*)
He apprehends a world of figures here,
But (*antithesis*) not the form of what he should attend.

(*Henry IV Part One*, 1.2.199–208)[11]

His uncle, Worcester, dismisses his nephew's speech as nothing more than rhetorical hot air, a 'world of figures.'

In addition to rhetorical skill, Shakespeare's plays bristle with proverbial knowledge. Open any edition of a single Shakespeare play worth its salt and you should find the proverbs and aphorisms glossed and referenced. There is a highly entertaining sentence constructed by Bernard Levin that purports to be made up of words and phrases that Shakespeare invented but it should be approached with caution.[12] Shakespeare was using many sayings that were already available to him and Levin's clever sentence represents a rhetorical sleight of hand.

Having immersed ourselves in rhetorical learning and proverbial wisdom, we might try to assemble an approximation of Shakespeare's library around us and read what we know he read. Each new play involved research and his work is the product of study and reflection. We would need to read in the original Latin (or in Arthur Golding's 1567 English translation) Ovid's *Metamorphoses* for *Venus and Adonis*. Young Lucius brings a copy of the Ovid on to the stage in *Titus Andronicus* (4.1.); Innogen is reading from it in *Cymbeline* (2.2.); Prospero quotes from it in *The Tempest* (5.1.). We would know Ovid's mythological and poetic histories in the *Fasti* (for *The Rape of Lucrece*); Virgil's *Aeneid* (for *Troilus and Cressida* and the place of Troy in Shakespeare's imagination, for example in *Hamlet*); Plautus's comedies *Menaechmi* and *Amphitryon* (for *The Comedy of Errors*), and Seneca's ten surviving plays (whose brutality and violence helped to make possible *Titus Andronicus*, the bloodiest play). From Roman comedies he learnt about the stock dramatic characters, such as the old man who desires a young woman, the angry wife, the courtesan, and the braggart soldier, all comic tropes evident in *The Taming of the Shrew*, *The Comedy of Errors*, and *All's Well That Ends Well*. We would need to read the Greek historian Plutarch's account of the lives of great men (which Shakespeare used for his Roman plays *Julius Caesar, Antony and Cleopatra, Coriolanus* and *Timon of Athens*). We could read Plutarch in English, in the 1595 translation by Sir Thomas North, as Shakespeare did.

From much closer to Shakespeare's own time we would certainly read the fourteenth-century poet John Gower's 33,000-line Middle English poem *Confessio Amantis* (especially for *Pericles*) and Geoffrey Chaucer's *The Canterbury Tales* (for *A Midsummer Night's Dream* and *The Two Noble Kinsmen*) and his *Troilus and Criseyde* (for *Troilus and*

Cressida). William Painter's *Palace of Pleasure* (from 1575) included a version of the story of *All's Well That Ends Well* (based on the fourteenth-century Italian Giovanni Boccaccio's *Decameron*). We would have to immerse ourselves in Raphael Holinshed's *Chronicles of England, Scotland and Ireland* (for all of the history plays – which make up about a third of Shakespeare's total output – as well as for *King Lear*, *Macbeth* and *Cymbeline*), and Edward Hall's chronicle *The Union of the Two Noble and Illustrious Families of Lancaster and York* (especially for the plays dealing with the Wars of the Roses: the three parts of *Henry VI* and *Richard III*).

The Portuguese writer Jorge de Montemayor's *Diana* (partly translated by 1563) for *The Two Gentlemen of Verona*; George Gascoigne's early comedy *Supposes* (based on an Italian source from 1509 and published in 1573), for *The Taming of the Shrew*; and George Whetstone's tragi-comedy *Promus and Cassandra* (from 1578), for *Measure for Measure*, would all need to be on our list, as would Sir John Harington's 1591 translation of the late fifteenth-century Italian poet Ariosto's *Orlando Furioso* (for *Much Ado About Nothing*).

In the original Italian we would read (as Shakespeare did) a collection of fifty short stories published in 1558 called *Il Pecorone* (*The Dunce*) for *The Merchant of Venice* and Giraldi Cinthio's *Gl'Ecatommiti* (*The One Hundred Tales*, from 1565) for *Othello*. In the original French, Shakespeare read François de Belleforest's *Histoires Tragiques* (from 1570) for *Hamlet*.

From Shakespeare's reading of contemporary English fiction, we would acquaint ourselves with Arthur Brooke's long poem *The Tragical History of Romeus and Juliet* (1562) and Thomas Lodge's *Rosalynde* (1590) for *As You Like It*. Barnaby Riche's collection of romantic stories *His Farewell to Military Profession* (1581) and Emmanuel Forde's novel *The Famous History of Parismus* (1598) were other important sources for *Twelfth Night, or What You Will* (as well as *Gl'Ingannati*, mentioned earlier). Sir Philip Sidney's prose work *Arcadia* (1593) provided source material for *King Lear*, as did the anonymous play, *The True Chronicle History of King Leir and his Three Daughters* (1605). Similarly, *The Famous Victories of Henry V* (1594) provided a source for *Henry IV Parts One* and *Two* and for *Henry V*. Later in his career, Shakespeare and his co-author, the brothel-keeper, George Wilkins, drew on Laurence Twine's *The Pattern of Painful Adventures* (from the mid-1570s) for *Pericles*, and Robert Greene's *Pandosto* (1588) is the source of *The Winter's Tale*.

We would read the Bible, regularly (especially the books of Genesis, Job, the Psalms and the New Testament). Shakespeare knew his Bible well and used it a lot. An act of parliament 'to restrain the abuses of players' prevented the word 'God' being used on stage from 1606 (when 'Jove' was often used as the alternative), and it was forbidden to dramatise Bible stories in the professional theatres. But Shakespeare's work is shot through with biblical allusions which shape some of his characterisations, for example the prodigal son Prince Harry in the two *Henry IV* plays, and there are Christ-like comparisons across the works, such as Richard II, and Cordelia in *King Lear*. It is perhaps surprising to learn that the character who quotes the Bible the most (inaccurately and never in any way to evangelise) is the drinking and whoring Sir John Falstaff.[13] We would familiarise ourselves, too, with the medieval mystery plays (short dramas based on the Bible performed by city craftsmen); and Michel de Montaigne's essays (John Florio's translation was published in 1603) would show us a contemporary, Renaissance mind reflecting on itself, as it were in soliloquy.

So far, our Shakespeare library contains biblical, classical, medieval and Renaissance literature from across Europe, which we need to be able to read in Latin, French and Italian, as well as in English. Four of the plays stand out for not having a single, major identifiable source – *A Midsummer Night's Dream*, *Love's Labour's Lost*, *The Merry Wives of Windsor* and *The Tempest* – because their narrative elements come from several different places. But the books mentioned here take us a long way to understanding the kind of reading that informed Shakespeare's imagination. Other sources and influences must be reasonably assumed: the travellers' tales he heard in cosmopolitan London as well as everything he saw, the spaces in which he spent his time, the people he knew and the conversations he had.

The London of Shakespeare's time was burgeoning with books that were helping to shape the culture in which he lived. The world's great Shakespeare and Renaissance libraries (the Folger in Washington, the Huntington in Los Angeles, the Bodleian in Oxford, the British Library in London and The Shakespeare Centre in Stratford-upon-Avon) contain between them thousands of books that were available for purchase on Elizabethan and Jacobean bookstalls. Some he read in their entirety and loved all his life, others he dipped into. He had, like many writers, a magpie mind that gathered morsels of all kinds with which to build a play. He read challengingly and diversely, had an excellent memory, and his reading stayed with him throughout his career.

BRIGHT STARS

Two early Renaissance writers dazzled their contemporaries shortly before Shakespeare came onto the scene: John Lyly (*c.*1554–1606) and Christopher Marlowe (1564–1593). Both men had a profound effect on him. Lyly's major works, which include both prose fiction and comedies, were published from the late 1570s and remained popular. His work taught Shakespeare how to write dramatic prose so that words became the focus of dramatic action, the plot yielding to conversation and argument, especially as in *Love's Labour's Lost*, *The Merry Wives of Windsor*, *Henry IV Parts One* and *Two* and *As You Like It*. Lyly's influence can be found in any Shakespearian character who likes to talk for the sake of it: the Nurse in *Romeo and Juliet*, Sir Toby Belch in *Twelfth Night, or What You Will*, and Autolycus in *The Winter's Tale* – to name but a few.

Christopher Marlowe, like Shakespeare, was the son of a tradesman, a shoemaker, and he imbibed his Latin literature at a new grammar school in Canterbury. Unlike Shakespeare, Marlowe then went on to university. His plays burst onto an astonished stage from the late 1580s and became popular. 'Marlowe's mighty line' (as Ben Jonson called it) has a memorable and ingratiating poetic sound all of its own and worked its magic upon Shakespeare's imagination. There are close affinities between Marlowe's erotic poem *Hero and Leander* (published posthumously in 1598) and Shakespeare's *Venus and Adonis* (published in 1593, which suggests he knew Marlowe's poem in manuscript); between Marlowe's play about a weak king, *Edward II*, and Shakespeare's *Richard II*; and between Marlowe's satire *The Jew of Malta* and Shakespeare's *The Merchant of Venice*.

The effect of Marlowe's many mighty moments deeply influenced Shakespeare, for example when the scholar-magician Dr Faustus glimpses Helen of Troy just moments before his eternal damnation:

FAUSTUS
Was this the face that launched a thousand ships
And burnt the topless towers of Ilium?
Sweet Helen, make me immortal with a kiss.
[*They kiss.*]
Her lips suck forth my soul. See where it flies!
Come, Helen, come, give me my soul again.
[*They kiss again.*]
Here will I dwell, for heaven be in these lips,
And all is dross that is not Helena.

(*Dr Faustus*, scene 13, 90–7).[14]

This episode haunted Shakespeare throughout his career. When Romeo and Juliet first meet at the Capulet ball, we hear and see:

ROMEO
Sin from my lips? O trespass sweetly urged!
Give me my sin again.

(*Romeo and Juliet*, 1.5.108–9)

The kiss is sweet and seals the inevitability of Romeo and Juliet's tragedy. Shakespeare is thinking of Marlowe's Dr Faustus when the dethroned Richard II stares at his own reflection in a looking glass:

> Was this face the face
> That every day under his household roof
> Did keep ten thousand men? Was this the face
> That like the sun did make beholders wink?
> Is this the face which faced so many follies,
> That was at last outfaced by Bolingbroke?
> A brittle glory shineth in this face,
> As brittle as the glory is the face,
> *He shatters the glass*
> For there it is, cracked in an hundred shivers.

(*Richard II*, 4.1.273–79)

Years later, in *Troilus and Cressida*, Shakespeare brings the legendary Helen onto stage as well (3.1.), but satirises her as little more than a self-absorbed fool, hopelessly devoted to Prince Paris. Marlowe was a colourful and dangerous character, only two months older than Shakespeare: who knows what he might have produced had he not been killed during an argument over a tavern bill in Deptford on 30 May 1593, aged just 29? The excitement that Shakespeare found in Marlowe ignited and inspired his talent for playwriting. Although the two are distinctive dramatists stylistically, without Marlowe Shakespeare would have been very different.

SHAKESPEARE THE ALCHEMIST

Shakespeare always complicates his source material at the same time as adapting and reshaping it. In *Othello*, for example, he introduces questions of motive which are absent from the story as he found it in Cinthio's original. Has Othello slept with Iago's wife Emilia (*Othello*, 1.3.378–80, 2.1.294–99)? Is Iago in love with Desdemona (2.1.290–93), and is that why Iago plots to destroy Othello as cruelly as he does? The only character to be named in the source is 'Disdemona'. All the other names are invented by Shakespeare, including Iago (curiously, the Spanish version of James and the name of the king who commanded a royal performance of the play by the King's Men on All Saints' Day, 1 November 1604). At the end of Cinthio's crudely moralistic story one of the lessons to be learned is that parents should take great care in naming their children: 'Disdemona' means 'the unfortunate one' and Cinthio's moral warning conveys a 'and-look-what-happened-to-her' message.

What does happen to her in the source narrative? The Ensign (Iago) hides in the bedroom wardrobe and makes a noise. The Moor (Othello) tells Disdemona to investigate. The Ensign appears and beats her on the back of the head with a sand-filled stocking. He and the Moor then break her skull, causing the bedroom ceiling to collapse in an attempt to make it look like an accidental death. In contrast Shakespeare has Desdemona fight for her life – 'Kill me tomorrow; let me live tonight' (*Othello*, 5.2.87) – and has Othello *alone* smothering her to death in a quasi-erotic suffocation. Shakespeare, in contrast to his source story, does not allow a single drop of her blood to be shed, his Othello taking great care that her unbroken skin remains icon-like 'and smooth as monumental alabaster' (*Othello*, 5.2.5). Chillingly, Shakespeare's Othello already sees Desdemona as an effigy on a tomb by the time he arrives to murder her.

Sometimes it is possible to imagine Shakespeare with his source book open in front of him, transforming the words to convey a much richer experience of thought and feeling. Here is Holinshed's account of Henry V's speech as he rallies the hopelessly outnumbered English troops into battle against the French at Agincourt:

> I would not wish a man more than I have; we are indeed in comparison to the enemies but a few, but if God of his clemency do favour us and our just cause, as I trust he will, we shall speed well enough. But let no man ascribe victory to our own strength and might but only to God's assistance, to whom I have no doubt we shall worthily have cause to give thanks therefore. And if so be that for our offences' sakes we shall be delivered into the hands of our enemies, the less number we be, the less damage shall the realm of England sustain.

Shakespeare adds the emotional and rhetorical emphases of the battle being fought on St Crispin's Day (25 October) and has his King Henry encouraging his troops to imagine the anniversary of the day in years to come and to think of themselves memorably as 'we few, we happy few, we band of brothers' (*Henry V*, 4.3.40–67, line 60). Interesting, too, is how Holinshed places greater stress on the king and his men calling directly on God's assistance. In contrast, Shakespeare's Henry V evokes the medieval, Roman Catholic sensibility and calls for the support of Saint Crispin (the patron saint of shoemakers, as it happens).

His treatment of Cleopatra also provides valuable insights into how he worked. Here is Plutarch's description of Cleopatra in her barge from North's translation:

> To take her barge to the edge of the river Cydnus, the poop whereof was of gold, the sails of purple, and the oars of silver, which kept stroke in rowing after the sound of the music of flutes, howboys, citherns, viols, and such other instruments as they played upon in the barge. And now for the person of herself: she was laid under a pavilion of cloth of gold of tissue, apparelled and attired like the goddess Venus commonly drawn in picture; and hard by her, on either hand of her, pretty fair boys apparelled as painters do set forth the god Cupid, with little fans in their hands, with the which they fanned wind upon her. Her ladies and gentlewomen also, the fairest of them were apparelled like the nymphs Nereides (which are the mermaids of the waters) and like the Graces, some steering the helm, others tending the tackle and ropes of the barge, out of which there came a wonderful passing sweet savour of perfumes, that perfumed the wharf's side, pestered with innumerable multitudes of people. Some of them followed the barge all alongst the river's side; others also ran out of the city to see her coming in; so that in the end there ran such multitudes of people one after another to see her that Antonius was left post-alone in the market place in

his imperial seat to give audience. And there went a rumour in the people's mouths that the goddess Venus was come to play with the god Bacchus, for the general good of all Asia.

Plutarch is keen to describe the colours, clothing, scent and music as well as the other people who are on the barge with Cleopatra – her pageboys, like little love-gods, and her waiting gentlewomen – and those running along the riverbank. The moment is already intricately and richly described before Shakespeare turns his mind to it. But he brings about a poetic metamorphosis. He follows the source closely but heightens Cleopatra's exceptional magnetism by transforming Plutarch's rich prose into golden verse:

ENOBARBUS
The barge she sat in, like a burnished throne,
Burned on the water. The poop was beaten gold;
Purple the sails, and so perfumèd that
The winds were love-sick with them. The oars were silver,
Which to the tune of flutes kept stroke, and made
The water which they beat to follow faster,
As amorous of their strokes. For her own person,
It beggared all description. She did lie
In her pavilion – cloth of gold, of tissue –
O'er-picturing that Venus where we see
The fancy outwork nature. On each side her
Stood pretty dimpled boys, like smiling Cupids,
With divers-coloured fans whose wind did seem
To glow the delicate cheeks which they did cool,
And what they undid did.
AGRIPPA   O, rare for Antony!
ENOBARBUS
Her gentlewomen, like the Nereides,
So many mermaids, tended her i'th'eyes,

And made their bends adornings. At the helm
A seeming mermaid steers. The silken tackle
Swell with the touches of those flower-soft hands
That yarely frame the office. From the barge
A strange invisible perfume hits the sense
Of the adjacent wharfs. The city cast
Her people out upon her, and Antony,
Enthroned i'th'market-place, did sit alone,
Whistling to th'air, which but for vacancy
Had gone to gaze on Cleopatra too,
And made a gap in nature.

(*Antony and Cleopatra*, 2.2.198–224)

Shakespeare re-casts Plutarch entirely as lyrical poetry and enhances it with the emphatic musical sounds of 'burnished' and 'burned', and the breathless plosive and alliterative excitement of 'poop' (the stern of the barge), 'purple' and 'perfumèd'. Shakespeare is captivated by the effect that Cleopatra and her barge have on the natural elements – the wind itself is 'love-sick' – and he takes us erotically close to the 'glow' of her 'delicate cheeks', presenting the moment as enigmatic and sexually charged. The ship's 'silken tackle' swells in the quick ('yarely') hands of Cleopatra's women. The fans used to cool Egypt's famous queen have the contradictory effect of keeping her warm. He does not refer to the classical gods Venus (goddess of love) and Bacchus (god of wine) and emphasises the natural world instead. The air itself has created 'a gap in nature', a sort of vacuum, and has gone to see Cleopatra too, while Shakespeare's Antony is left whistling in the marketplace. Plutarch's account is a careful and colourful commentary on a live event; Shakespeare produces a burnished oil painting: lyrical, erotic, enigmatic.

AMONG THE ACTORS

As well as books, Shakespeare needed actors. They illuminated his words and kept the audience wanting more. Throughout much of his career, Shakespeare produced plays for a stable company of actors who became old friends. He knew how they would deliver his lines, speak the poetry and crack the jokes. The company formed in 1594, stayed together, and the characters in the plays aged with them. Richard Burbage (1568–1619) tended to take the leading roles and audiences were able to watch him grow from Richard III and Hamlet through to Othello and King Lear, while Shakespeare was writing these major roles for someone who was roughly the same age as himself.

There are moments in some of the printed plays in which names of actors are accidentally used instead of the speech-prefixes of the characters. So, for example, in the edition of *Much Ado About Nothing* published in 1600, the names of the much-loved comedians Will Kemp and Richard Cowley appear instead of their roles Dogberry and Verges, indicating that Shakespeare was writing as much with the actors in mind as the characters they were playing. This slippage between actor and role also suggests that the printed version of *Much Ado About Nothing* was based on Shakespeare's own (now lost) manuscript.

Actors were not given a full script but only their actual

speeches with the cue-lines. They knew the line just before their own and had to listen out carefully for it, a practice which gave an immediate, almost improvisatory quality to the style of acting. Shakespeare jokes about this in *A Midsummer Night's Dream* when the workmen of Athens are rehearsing their play, 'Pyramus and Thisbe': 'You speak all your part at once, cues and all' says their long-suffering director figure, Peter Quince, to Francis Flute, the bellows-mender (*A Midsummer Night's Dream*, 2.2.93–4).

Writing for a company of actors whose abilities he knew intimately and with whom he rehearsed explains why there are only sparse stage directions in the early printed texts. Quite often these are only implied in the dialogue: 'See, it stalks away' says Barnardo of Hamlet's father's ghost (*Hamlet*, 1.1.48); 'You must not kneel' says Cordelia to her aged father, King Lear (*The Tragedy of King Lear*, 4.6.52), implying that he tries to do so on the line before; 'he cares not for your weeping' says Volumnia to Coriolanus's wife, Virgilia (*Coriolanus*, 5.3.157). In *Henry IV Part One* there are the directions, '*the lady speaks in Welsh*', for example (3.1.193), and a little later '*here the lady sings a Welsh song*' (3.1.240.1). Shakespeare did not have to (and probably could not) provide the Welsh dialogue or song, but the fact that the moment is there suggests there was an actor in the company who could be relied on to write, speak and sing it.

Physical descriptions help determine casting. Hermia in *A Midsummer Night's Dream*, for example, should be short of stature (Lysander calls her a 'dwarf', a 'bead', an 'acorn' 3.2.329 and 331) whereas her counterpart Helena is tall. Hermia taunts Helena by calling her a 'painted maypole'

(3.2.290–97). You need to be extremely thin to play Dr Pinch in *The Comedy of Errors*, 'a hungry lean-faced villain' (5.1.238) and, as his name implies, Sir Andrew Aguecheek in *Twelfth Night, or What You Will*, so it is likely that the same actor played both roles. It helps if the actor playing Falstaff is naturally fat (padding can help, but often does not ring true in performance). But on the whole, Shakespeare's scripts are blessedly free from over-determined instructions. You do not have to be old in order to play King Lear (Burbage was only around forty) because he describes himself as 'four score and upward' (*The Tragedy of King Lear*, 4.6.54); you just have to convince the audience. Shakespeare knew the actors' talents, wrote according to their abilities, and entrusted his words to their interpretative action. This is why directors over the centuries have rejoiced in the friendliness, understanding, and freedom that they find in Shakespeare's work, a text for actors.

The Shakespearian stage was bare but included a few vital components: three entrances and exits including the middle, curtained 'discovery space' (essential for eavesdroppers, and the place, for example, where Polonius in *Hamlet* is murdered, 'behind the arras', 3.4.22.1). Entrances and exits on either side of it allow for a character or a group of characters to leave just as others enter from the opposite side. It might be a twin who just misses seeing his or her brother or sister (in *The Comedy of Errors* or *Twelfth Night, or What You Will*), or an opposing character, or even an army. The stage was never cluttered with scenery and did not require elaborate set changes. The emphasis was on fluidity and pace, one scene melting quickly into another with an energetic sense of continuous action. There was a trapdoor (from which ghosts might appear and where graves could be dug), and an upper playing space (from which gods might descend and where lovers could enjoy a privileged focal point).

From 1608, when the King's Men took over the running of the indoor Blackfriars Theatre, Shakespeare could rely on a more intimate playing space than at The Globe. The audience were all seated and there was scope for lighting effects with candles. *The Tempest* seems to have been written especially for this indoor venue because it requires more special effects than any of the other plays (for example the spirit Ariel in flight, the sudden appearance of a magical banquet, and the descent of three goddesses). Its long, subtle scenes suggest that Shakespeare was writing it with an intimate playing space in mind. Being primarily written for the Blackfriars Theatre would not have precluded performances at 'the great [G]lobe itself' (*The Tempest*, 4.1.153), though probably with modified action. The arraignment of Queen Katherine of Aragon during the divorce proceedings of Henry VIII had actually taken place in the Blackfriars. When Shakespeare and Fletcher's play *All is True* (*Henry VIII*) was performed there, that particular scene (2.4.) would have taken on a special resonance in its site-specific venue. The script, too, was closely based on the words spoken at the royal hearing. But we know that the play was performed at the Globe as well (rather like a play in our own time which opens in a small, niche, studio space and then transfers to a much bigger venue). Henry VIII infamously dissolved the monasteries and great religious houses; the play about him literally set the Globe on fire and burned it to the ground.

All of Shakespeare's plays can be performed with a basic company of ten men and three boys, supplemented by 'hired-men' when needed. Parts needed to be doubled (and more, in the early history plays especially), but Shakespeare's plotting allows for this. Boys, not men, played the female roles, helped by the fact that their voices broke later than male voices do now. The records at Durham and Chichester cathedrals for the 1560s show that some boys could still sing treble as late as sixteen, old enough to have the emotional intelligence to perform one of Shakespeare's great female roles.[15] A sixteen-year-old boy could bring precisely the right kind of petulance, sexual capriciousness and flirtation to the role of Cleopatra, or even imitate the devouring mother, Volumnia, in *Coriolanus*.

Shakespeare made use of the fact that boys played the female roles to create dizzying dramatic effects. While seeking to make his audience erotically aware of Cleopatra, he wants us to be aware of the boy player inhabiting the part. Just moments before her suicide Cleopatra stares into a terrible future without Antony in which she imagines Caesar taking her as a prisoner back to Rome. She fears that the workmen of Rome will mock her on the stage:

> Antony
> Shall be brought drunken forth, and I shall see
> Some squeaking Cleopatra boy my greatness
> I'th' posture of a whore.

> (*Antony and Cleopatra*, 5.2.214–17)

Our attention is drawn to the boy player in the role of Cleopatra at the same time as Cleopatra imagines another boy player playing her. Henry Jackson of Corpus Christi College, Oxford, saw the King's Men perform *Othello* there in 1610. His eyewitness account (in Latin) provides valuable evidence about the impact a boy actor could make:

> the celebrated Desdemona, slain in our presence by her husband, although she pleaded her case very effectively throughout, yet moved us more after she was dead, when, lying in her bed, she entreated the pity of the spectators by her very countenance.

Jackson clearly found his performance captivating and this particular, anonymous boy was obviously a star in his own right.

SUPPLY AND DEMAND

Shakespeare was aware of his audience's tastes, which shifted and developed over time. It becomes easy to imagine meetings of the company's co-shareholders in which the next kind of play was debated before Shakespeare wrote it. *Henry V*, for example, which glorifies a head of state, is followed by *Julius Caesar* about an assassination. He was to some extent always writing to commission. There is a marked shift in dramatic tone between Elizabethan and Jacobean Shakespeare when, from 1603, he effectively became the royal playwright. There are no more explicitly romantic comedies after *Twelfth Night, or What You Will* (in 1601) and thereafter Shakespeare produced a much darker dramatic texture in plays such as *Troilus and Cressida, Measure for Measure,*

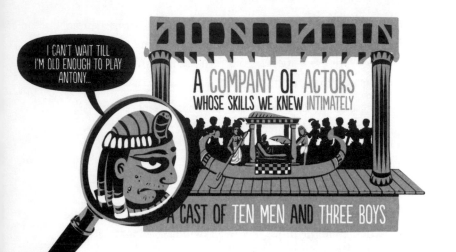

All's Well That Ends Well, and then a cluster of tragedies. James I's fascination with witchcraft and the supernatural prompted *Macbeth*, a play that also reminded the monarch of his Scottish ancestry and his descent from the line of Banquo ('your children shall be kings', *Macbeth* 1.3.83). And it was the Jacobean court that had a taste for what became known as tragi-comedy, exemplified by plays such as *The Winter's Tale*, *Cymbeline* and *The Two Noble Kinsmen*.

State censorship was an important shaping factor. The most vital, illustrative document is the manuscript of *The Book of Sir Thomas More*, a collaborative play of the 1590s, understood to be by Antony Munday and Henry Chettle, but transcribed by Munday, probably in 1600, and into which have been inserted revisions apparently by Thomas Dekker, Thomas Heywood and William Shakespeare. [16] Crucially, the manuscript also shows us how Shakespeare wrote. The principal passage thought to be by Shakespeare is lightly punctuated, perhaps in the first draft of composition, and the handwriting bears comparison with his six surviving signatures, notably the 'distinctive "spurred" form of the letter "a"'.[17] Marked into it are the only surviving interventions by Edmund Tilney, the Master of the Revels, the official in charge of ensuring that plays did not contain politically sensitive or overtly religious material. It looks like Tilney was dissatisfied with the portrayal of the May Day riots against foreigners and any mention of the Oath of Succession, which More could not accept. Tilney, it seems, held on to the manuscript, forbidding both performance and publication.

COLLABORATION, REVISION AND AUTHORSHIP

One of the most significant developments in Shakespeare scholarship since the 1980s has been a growing understanding of how Shakespeare collaborated, a common practice among all of his contemporaries (Thomas Heywood, for example, claimed to have 'a main finger' in around 220 plays). The example of *Sir Thomas More* shows Shakespeare being brought in to patch up an already existing script, but he is also thought to have collaborated on several other plays, mainly at the beginning and end of his career. Based on stylometric tests designed to reveal different hands at work in the same play the theories – and they are only theories – about how Shakespeare collaborated reveal different kinds of practice. In *Henry VI Part One* (with Thomas Nashe), *Titus Andronicus* (with George Peele), and *Timon of Athens* (with Thomas Middleton), the collaborating dramatist seems to have contributed a few scenes within a particular act (in the case of *Titus Andronicus* the whole of act one). In *Pericles*, George Wilkins seems to have written the first half and Shakespeare the second (from scene 11). The scenes with Hecate, the Queen of the witches, in *Macbeth* (3.4. and 4.1.) include material which refers to Thomas Middleton's play *The Witch* which suggests he adapted the play, at least in part, before it found its way into the Folio of 1623. It has been suggested that Middleton's hand can be seen at work in *Measure for Measure* (supplying act one, scene two and possibly altering the end of act three and the beginning of act four). The later plays show a different model of collaboration in which the labour has been divided more equally into definite stints across the whole of the drama. Since the nineteenth century, John Fletcher's hand has been identified in *All is True* (*Henry VIII*), and there is external evidence that tells us he collaborated with Shakespeare on *The Two Noble Kinsmen* and the lost play *Cardenio*. Perhaps when working with Fletcher in this way, Shakespeare was the thought leader and innovator of style, encouraging Fletcher to take on the role of the leading dramatist for the King's Men.

Several plays have been known variously over the centuries as 'the Shakespeare Apocrypha', 'doubtful' or even 'dubious' works, in which Shakespeare may or may not have had a hand. The term 'apocryphal' evokes the canon of holy writ against which writing is measured for inclusion or exclusion. Knowing more about Shakespeare as a collaborative playwright has led to a renewed interest in these plays and the list has fluctuated over time. A useful distinction can be drawn here between 'contributed' and 'collaborated'. Shakespeare's hand in them, if present at all, seems to be intermittent and not part of an overall artistic design. Two of these plays, *The London Prodigal* and *A Yorkshire Tragedy*, name Shakespeare as the author on their title pages. Both were performed by the King's Men, which may partly explain why his name is there. Or it might have been added by the publisher eager to encourage sales. *Edward III* however, which used to be among this category of play, can now be found jacketed and canonised among the major Shakespeare editions. One theory suggests that Shakespeare wrote up to four of its eighteen scenes.

Shakespeare revised his work. For half of the plays we only have one text, the Folio version of 1623. The other half exists in at least two versions, the Folio and the earlier quarto texts. For many years, it was assumed that each text had come down to us imperfectly, representing a lost original. But modern scholarship understands the different versions to be a result of authorial revision, sometimes minor (in the case of *A Midsummer Night's Dream* which reallocates some of the speeches), sometimes more significant. There are three significantly different versions of *Hamlet*, and two of *King Lear*, *Othello* and *Troilus and Cressida*. Shakespeare's revisions included abridgement but mainly affected the adjustment and enhancement of the dramatic texture. For example, the later, Folio version of *King Lear* is even more uncompromisingly harsh: there are no servants who come forward to apply whites of eggs to the bleeding eye-sockets of the tortured and blinded Earl of Gloucester (as they do in the earlier *The History of King Lear,* scene 14, 104–5). The Folio version of *Othello* amplifies the role of the foppish Roderigo as a foil for Iago and only in the Folio does Desdemona sing 'a song of willow' about love forsaken in the scene before she is murdered. Her music brings an emphatic and haunting stillness to the moment. Only in the Folio do Desdemona and Emilia then go on to talk candidly about marital infidelity and the duty that wives owe their husbands (4.3.).

That Shakespeare wrote for actors he knew, collaborated with other playwrights, and revised his work in light of theatrical contingencies should give us pause before giving any credence to theories which claim that someone else was the author of the plays. Besides the obvious biographical and historical objections (these theories have to reject the evidence of Shakespeare's memorial bust in Holy Trinity Church and the Folio of 1623), the plays attributed to and written by William Shakespeare of Stratford-upon-Avon were not written in a vacuum. They needed the playhouse, the actors, the theatrical climate and industry of the time in order to be produced. It is simplistic and wrong-headed to suppose that they could have been written in isolation by an aristocrat, for example, which many of the theories attempt to prove. Some people even argue that Christopher Marlowe did not die in 1593 but instead stayed alive, secretly writing the works of Shakespeare. But his death was certified by a coroner and independent witnesses, and his burial recorded in the register of St Nicholas's Church, Deptford. People who argue that Shakespeare did not write

Shakespeare are sometimes known as anti-Stratfordians, but in 2013 I co-coined a new term: 'anti-Shakespearian'. Since no artist can be separated from the social context that helped to form and sustain his or her creativity, it is as illogical to separate Stratford-upon-Avon from Shakespeare as it is, for example, to separate Michelangelo from Florence and Rome. The term anti-Shakespearian is therefore a more accurate description of the Shakespeare deniers' agenda.[18] While it is fascinating to appreciate the anti-Shakespearian endeavours as a psychological and cultural phenomenon, beginning in the mid-nineteenth century around the same time as the rise of detective fiction and Charles Darwin's theories of natural origins, they have nothing to do with how playwrights of Shakespeare's period actually wrote.

NEVER BLOTTING A LINE?

'Fantastic!', the Hollywood film producer Samuel Goldwyn is said to have remarked, 'and it was all written with a feather!' It is worth thinking about Shakespeare's feather for a moment and the practicalities of writing in his time. Quill pens needed good ink to help prevent blotting. The nib would need proper stiffening by being dipped into cold water and then into hot sand and sharpening every so often. The dipping into the ink had to be done carefully, evenly and steadily. The ink itself was usually home-made from oak apples, that is the crushed, empty chrysalis husks which the grubs of oak trees leave behind when they have turned into wasps, along with gum Arabic for a fixative, and mixed with rainwater, vinegar or wine so that it flowed sufficiently and did not blot.

We know Shakespeare was right-handed, but we do not know how many nibs he used to write a play, or how often he sharpened it, or who made his ink. But his friends and fellow actors, John Heminges and Henry Condell (who put together the first major collection of Shakespeare's plays, the Folio of 1623) portray Shakespeare as a natural writer whose thought and written expression were one: 'his mind and hand went together, and what he thought he uttered with that easiness that we have scarce received from him a blot in his papers.' Their description summons up an image of Shakespeare writing swiftly and gracefully. Characteristically, though, Ben Jonson is on hand to puncture and contradict any suggestion of idyllic composition. In the posthumously published *Timber* (written in 1630), he writes: 'I remember the players have often mentioned it as an honour to Shakespeare that in his writing, whatsoever he penned, he never blotted out line. My answer hath been, "Would he had blotted a thousand," which they thought a malevolent speech. I had not told posterity this but for their ignorance, who chose that circumstance to commend their friend by, wherein he most faulted.' Perhaps all three men are telling different sides of the same truth. Heminges and Condell could be referring to manuscripts in fair copy that they worked with; Jonson, as well as suggesting that Shakespeare should have had a greater sense of self-censorship and restraint, also sounds as though he knew how Shakespeare wrote, had watched him write, and saw him crossing out.

If pushed to suggest one role that Shakespeare himself played in his works (though there is no evidence to show which he did actually perform), I would nominate the Chorus in *Henry V*, because of the way it reminds us of the powers of the imagination and the process of playwriting. In the Chorus's sonnet-Epilogue we hear:

> Thus far with rough and all-unable pen
> Our bending author hath pursued the story,
> In little room confining mighty men,
> Mangling by starts the full course of their glory.

(Henry V, Epilogue, 1–4)

Were these lines spoken by Shakespeare himself as he opened his arms to a full house and took a bow as that same 'bending author'? He knew what it was to adapt a story of great scale into a drama of around two to three hours,

ALL THIS WITH A QUILL PEN AND HOME-MADE INK

and he knew what a messy business writing can be, especially with all of the surrounding professional and personal demands on his craft and concentration. But what was the work that came from his 'rough and all unable pen'?

3
WHAT DID HE WRITE?

A glance at the title page of the 1623 Folio immediately tells the reader and potential purchaser that the volume contains different kinds of plays: *Master William Shakespeare's Comedies, Histories and Tragedies*. A few pages further in and we come across 'a Catalogue', or list of contents, which divides the plays up into the three different classifications. John Heminges and Henry Condell were seeking to organise their late friend and colleague's works as attractively and helpfully as possible by dividing them up into three different genres that their audiences and readers would recognise.

But Heminges and Condell's organisation creates problems. Thankful as posterity is for their great labour of love, their generic divisions have become ingrained in the way we think about Shakespeare. Consistently he seems rather to have enjoyed challenging his audience's expectations of genre. He includes comic elements in tragedies and gestures towards the ingredients of tragedies in comedies (for example, by referring to, or including, deaths as part of the narrative).

Some of the plays resist easy categorisation. *Troilus and Cressida* and *Cymbeline* are placed among the tragedies in the Folio whereas both of them have strong claims to be known as comedies, or even histories. The former is Shakespeare's biting and satirical debunking of Greek and

Trojan heroes; the latter is a romantic and miraculous history play, based on Holinshed's chronicles. If *Cymbeline* is a tragedy because it contains the death of one of its characters, Prince Cloten (whose death is only really tragic for Cloten himself), then *The Winter's Tale*, which is found among the comedies, could be placed among the tragedies since it too includes a prince, Mamillius and a courtier, Antigonus, who die. *Henry VI Part Three*, *Richard III* and *Richard II* are history plays cast in tragic form; *Henry V* ends in marriage (its long final scene in which King Henry woos Princess Katherine takes that part of the play into the genre of comedy); *King Lear*, *Coriolanus*, *Julius Caesar*, *Timon of Athens* and *Antony and Cleopatra* are tragedies about historical figures.

First and foremost, Shakespeare was writing lively, entertaining, innovative and challenging plays. Generic considerations were secondary to him. This is why, if we take only the classical considerations of genre to Shakespeare, he will challenge them. Not for him the literary rules or theories of Horace and Aristotle. His project was altogether freer and more individual, so that the more Heminges and Condell's generic divisions are scrutinised, the less satisfactory they become. The King of France dies towards the end of the comedy *Love's Labour's Lost* (and one of the Princess's ladies-in-waiting

IT'S WHAT HE WOULD HAVE WANTED

HENRY CONDELL

GOOD FRIEND FOR JESUS
TO DIGG THE DUST EN
BLESE BE YE MAN YT SPA
AND CURST BE HE YT M

mentions her sister who died of love, 5.2.14–15). Ragasine, the pirate, dies in the comedy *Measure for Measure*. And the tragedies have their fair share of humorous figures: the drunken Porter in *Macbeth* (2.3.); the gravediggers in *Hamlet* (5.1.); the hapless clown who is put to death by the Emperor Saturninus in *Titus Andronicus* (4.4.40–49); the bawdy clown in *Othello* (3.1.1–29); and an obsessive, sinister clown who brings Cleopatra the poisonous asp in a basket of figs (*Antony and Cleopatra* 5.2.238–74).

In hindsight, it would have been far more useful to us if Heminges and Condell had printed the plays chronologically, since many of them are difficult to date. Unfortunately, chronology did not matter to them. Shakespeare's last sole-authored play, *The Tempest*, is printed first. Perhaps Heminges and Condell saw it as his great culmination as a dramatist. The history plays are arranged according to the historical order of their eponymous monarchs, rather than the order in which he wrote them. The *Henry VI* plays were written first; *Henry VI Part One* was written as a prequel after the composition of *Henry VI Part Two* and *Henry VI Part Three*, whose earliest titles were quite different (see 'A Chronology of Shakespeare's Works' at the front of this book). A chronological ordering of Shakespeare's plays is attempted by *The Oxford Shakespeare: The Complete Works* (1986; second edition 2005), presenting a richly suggestive way of appreciating his growth as a poet and professional dramatist.

GETTING UNDER SHAKESPEARE'S SKIN

The Two Gentlemen of Verona is possibly Shakespeare's earliest single-authored play, a suggestion supported by long stretches of inactivity for some characters, as though he forgot all about them. In act two, scene four, for example, Sir Thurio (a hapless role all round) remains silent for 79 lines and the witty servant, Speed, for 183, while the main drama takes place in front of them: the Duke, his daughter Silvia, and Valentine welcome Proteus (Valentine's friend) to the court of Milan.

Though minor in comparison to what was to follow, *The Two Gentlemen of Verona* bears careful reading because here we can see Shakespeare finding his feet as a dramatist, bodying forth ideas, techniques and situations that would feed into his later works. In what follows I look for Shakespeare's DNA as a writer: characterisation, dramatic situations, stagecraft and poetic expression that would find further expression throughout his career. *The Two Gentlemen of Verona* shows us how Shakespeare is in part always sourced in 'Shakespeare'. Like Johann Sebastian Bach, he was a great recycler of his own work, but always inflecting it differently each time around.

Two of Shakespeare's first female characters, Julia and her maid Lucetta, meet to talk about rival suitors. Kate and Bianca will do the same in *The Taming of the Shrew* (2. 1.), as will Portia and Nerissa in *The Merchant of Venice* (1.2.), and Cressida and her servant Alexander in *Troilus and Cressida* (1.2.). Desdemona and Emilia will compare tales about the qualities of husbands in *Othello* (4.3). Julia's decision to disguise herself as a boy and to visit Proteus in Milan makes her the first of the boys playing women to disguise themselves as boys or young men. Julia becomes Proteus's pageboy, sees him in love with Silvia, and has to convey tokens of love between them. Shakespeare uses this same plot device to provide sexual and emotional tensions for Rosalind in *As You Like It* and Viola in *Twelfth Night, or What You Will*. In *The Merchant of Venice*, Portia and Nerissa have more power as a result of their disguise, whereas Jessica in the same play and Innogen in *Cymbeline* use their disguise as boys in order to aid escape (Jessica from her father and Innogen from a plot to murder her).

The Two Gentlemen of Verona contains Shakespeare's first visual gag (and one of his best): the rope ladder that Valentine must hide about his person in front of the Duke so that he can successfully elope with the Duke's daughter, Silvia. The Duke knows about Valentine's plans (Valentine's 'friend' Proteus has betrayed him) so the episode is a game of cat and mouse, the rope ladder a farcical time bomb that the audience, with delighted anticipation, is waiting to be detonated. In a later play, the banished Romeo will use a rope ladder secretly to meet Juliet on their wedding night. Valentine's plot is uncovered, the hidden ladder discovered, and he is banished, but not before he speaks one of Shakespeare's most lovely and lyrical speeches:

> And why not death, rather than living torment?
> To die is to be banished from myself,
> And Silvia is myself. Banished from her
> Is self from self, a deadly banishment.
> What light is light, if Silvia be not seen?
> What joy is joy, if Silvia be not by?
> Unless it be to think that she is by,
> And feed upon the shadow of perfection.
> Except I be by Silvia in the night,
> There is no music in the nightingale.
> Unless I look on Silvia in the day
> There is no day for me to look upon.
> She is my essence, and I leave to be
> If I be not by her fair influence
> Fostered, illumined, cherished, kept alive.
> I fly not death, to fly his deadly doom.
> Tarry I here I but attend on death,
> But fly I hence, I fly away from life.

(*The Two Gentlemen of Verona*, 3.1.170–87)

The musicality of the verse is compelling, especially because of the gentle echoes of 'night' and 'nightingale', 'essence' and 'influence'. In the 1998 film *Shakespeare in Love* it is Shakespeare himself whose ear is caught by his own lines when a newly arrived actor (who he thinks is a boy) speaks them. Valentine's emotional and intellectual difficulty – that the self is defined in part through another person – would find fuller expression in the reunion of the twins in *The Comedy of Errors* and in *Twelfth Night, or What You Will*, and the lovers in *A Midsummer Night's Dream*. Stories of banishment seem to have fascinated Shakespeare. Valentine's place in Silvia's affections is usurped by Proteus and he is banished. In *As You Like It* Duke Frederick usurps his brother, Duke Senior, and banishes him. In *The Tempest* Antonio usurps and banishes his brother, the magician Prospero. Bolingbroke is banished by Richard II, Romeo by the Prince of Verona, the Earl of Kent and Cordelia by King Lear, Timon of Athens goes into self-imposed misanthropic exile and, at opposite ends of Shakespeare's career, King Tarquin in *Lucrece* and Coriolanus are banished by the people of Rome.

The character of Proteus (whose name suggests he can change shape and therefore dissemble) represents the first of Shakespeare's Machiavels. These scheming figures were popular in plays and claimed cultural sanction from the Italian philosophy of Niccolò Machiavelli: all is fair in love and war. Proteus anticipates the more fully fledged Shakespearian schemers such as Richard of Gloucester in the second and third parts of *Henry VI* and *Richard III*, Philip the Bastard in *King John*, Falstaff in *The Merry Wives of Windsor*, Claudio in *Much Ado About Nothing*, Brutus in

Julius Caesar, Hamlet, Angelo in *Measure for Measure*, Iago in *Othello*, Macbeth, and Giacomo in *Cymbeline*. The speed with which Proteus decides he wants to forget Julia and instead take Silvia away from Valentine (apparently only moments after Proteus has arrived in Milan and seen Silvia, 2.4.190–212) anticipates the suddenness of King Leontes's notoriously inexplicable jealousy in a much later play, *The Winter's Tale*.

ONE MAN AND HIS DOG

Then there is Lance, the deadpan, clownish servant of Proteus. He appears on stage with his dog, Crab. One of the great pleasures of seeing any stage production of *The Two Gentlemen of Verona* is watching a real dog take part in the main action. Shakespeare's script accommodates anything that the dog might do. In answer to a question from Speed (Valentine's servant) about whether it will 'be a match' (a marriage) between Proteus and Julia, Lance replies:

LANCE Ask my dog. If he say 'Ay', it will. If he say 'No', it will. If he shake his tail and say nothing, it will.
SPEED The conclusion is, then, that it will.

(2.5.31–3)

Much later, the actor playing Lance has a gift of a monologue when he returns to tell us about how Crab cocked his leg against a gentlewoman's dress in the Duke's court:

He had not been there – bless the mark – a pissing-while but all the chamber smelled him. […] I, having been acquainted

with the smell before, knew it was Crab, and goes me to the
fellow that whips the dogs. 'Friend', quoth I, 'you mean to
whip the dog.' 'Ay, marry do I,' quoth he. 'You do him the
more wrong', quoth I, ''twas I did the thing you wot of.' He
makes me no more ado, but whips me out of the chamber.
How many masters would do this for his servant? Nay, I'll be
sworn I have sat in the stocks for puddings he hath stolen,
otherwise he had been executed. I have stood on the pillory
for geese he hath killed, otherwise he had suffered for't. (*To
Crab*) Thou think'st not of this now.

(The Two Gentlemen of Verona, 4.4.18–33)

Lance's humour is quintessentially Shakespearian because
of its unabashed description of a bodily function. A dog
peeing does not need to be anything more than it seems,
but the moment is touched with the warm sentimentality of
Lance's sympathy for the animal. It is a marvellous episode
that exemplifies Shakespeare's ability to tell a story and to
sketch a picture of an off-stage reality. He often describes
for us what we cannot see and which he cannot easily
dramatise. Biondello's comic description of Petruccio and
his horse's outrageous appearance and journey to church to
marry Kate (*The Taming of the Shrew*, 3.2.42–61); the Duke
of Clarence's account of his nightmare about being drowned
(*Richard III*, 1.4.9–63); Mercutio's fantastical observations about the 'fairies' midwife', Queen Mab (*Romeo and
Juliet*, 1.4.55–94); the First Lord's moving account of Jaques
crying and moralising about a wounded stag in the Forest of
Ardenne (*As You Like It*, 2.1.25–63); Hamlet's adventure narrative of being taken by pirates and his sneaking across the
ship's deck to exchange the fateful letter that Rosencrantz

and Guildenstern were carrying (*Hamlet*, 4.6.11–28 and 5.2.13–63); and the understated and terrible memory of dead King Duncan that haunts Lady Macbeth during her famous sleep-walking scene – 'yet who would have thought the old man to have had so much blood in him?' (*Macbeth*, 5.1.36–8) – are all other examples of Shakespeare's powerful off-stage pictures.

The passage about Crab the dog illustrates beautifully Shakespeare's use of prose. Only five plays (all histories) are written entirely in verse: *Henry VI Part Three*, *Richard II*, *King John*, the collaborative *Henry VI Part One* and *Edward III*. Elsewhere Shakespeare uses prose extensively and to great effect, often for servants and non-aristocratic figures, but not exclusively. In prose Shakespeare is differently eloquent, often humorous, moving and sentimental. Stylistically, Shakespeare's use of prose was to have a lasting effect on his dramatic verse. It is possible that he found he could write prose more quickly than verse and it is interesting that in the mid-1590s there is an explosion of prose in his plays. Perhaps the newly formed Lord Chamberlain's Men required several plays to be written as soon as possible in order to become established and popular. The play with the highest proportion of prose is *The Merry Wives of Windsor*; *Much Ado About Nothing* is a close runner-up. The verse in his early plays tends to be highly regular and rhetorically shaped. As Shakespeare's use of prose increased, so too did his ability to write verse which sounds more and more like prose, that is, when the verse flows onto the following line. This starts to happen as early as *Romeo and Juliet* (the Nurse's speech in 1.2.18–50 was set as prose in the first quarto edition, even though it is verse). The vivid, dramatic poetry of Hamlet's soliloquies was made possible by the profound effect that writing prose had on Shakespeare. So, Lance's speeches in *The Two Gentlemen of Verona* mark an important feature of Shakespeare's artistry.

PROBLEMATIC ENDINGS

The ending of *The Two Gentlemen of Verona* is characteristic of Shakespearian comedy. Order is restored. Marital bliss and new generations are anticipated. All of Shakespeare's comedies either end with or look forward to marriage (in the case of *Love's Labour's Lost* a year and a day later). But because Shakespeare always gives and questions at the same time, human problems remain. Proteus tries to rape Silvia in the forest, but Valentine suddenly appears and intervenes. Proteus apologises and Valentine offers Silvia to his 'friend'. Julia (still disguised as Proteus's page) painfully observes the scene, faints, and her true identity is revealed. 'There are, by this time,' remarked the critic Arthur Quiller-Couch, 'no gentlemen in Verona.'[19] The Duke arrives with Sir Thurio (his husband of choice for Silvia) and the outlaws who have taken them as prisoners. Sir Thurio steps forward to take Silvia as his bride, but Valentine intervenes again and threatens to kill him. The Duke applauds Valentine's spirit, gives Silvia back to him after all, pardons the outlaws (at Valentine's request), and the two couples look forward to being married on the same day. And all, apparently, leave the stage to live happily ever after. Little wonder, then, that in some productions, the relationship between the servant Lance and his pissing dog is portrayed as the most mutually loyal and genuinely loving one in the entire play.

Other problematic endings include: how far Kate might be speaking tongue in cheek when she proclaims her loyalty to her husband (*The Taming of the Shrew*, 5.2.141–84); Duke Orsino who has fallen in love with Viola disguised as a boy waiting to see if she is still as attractive to him when dressed as a woman in *Twelfth Night, or What You Will*; and Bertram having to take up Helen whom he has been forced to marry and who has tricked him into getting her pregnant in the ironically entitled *All's Well That Ends Well*. *Measure for Measure* used always to end with the marriage between Isabella and the Duke, but in Shakespeare's script she remains silent. John Barton's 1970 production for the Royal Shakespeare Company was, as far as anyone knows, the first time when Isabella seemed to be stunned rather than delighted by the Duke's offer. Since then productions of the play have explored different conclusions. The Duke hints at marriage to the novice Isabella three times in the final scene, but why should she accept him? He has manipulated her life and made her believe her brother has been executed. All she wants is to become a nun. Even *A Midsummer Night's Dream*, which seems to end happily, raises questions. We know that Demetrius can only love Helena because he has been doped by love-juice and that the happiness of their marriage will always rely on the fairy kingdom's magic.

The endings of Shakespeare tragedies are no less problematic than his comedies. Just as we might feel that there are questions to be raised about the future happiness promised by marriage, so too our emotions usually feel divided at the end of a Shakespearian tragedy. Rather than judge his characters, Shakespeare requires us to take on multiple perspectives. When the Earl of Kent and Edgar look upon the dying King Lear who enters carrying his dead daughter, the innocent Cordelia, they share the following exchange:

KENT   Is this the promised end?
EDGAR Or image of that horror?

(*The Tragedy of King Lear*, 5.3.238–9)

Two questions, and one answer to both is staring them in the face. But Kent and Edgar also invite us to compare the horror of the moment to the end of the world. To ask where Shakespeare's sympathies lie is to ask the wrong question. It is far more satisfying to experience the ending of a Shakespearian tragedy through the eyes of characters who experience it, to take upon ourselves *their* perspectives, to allow these to manipulate and inform our own: Cleopatra and her waiting gentlewomen Charmian and Iras as they prepare for their suicides, and Octavius Caesar as he returns to the monument too late and finds them dead; Horatio as he bears in mind the number of dead around the royal court of Denmark (Polonius, Ophelia, King Claudius, Queen Gertrude, Laertes, Rosencrantz, Guildenstern and Hamlet) and promises to tell their histories aright to the new-conquering Prince Fortinbras (*Hamlet*, 5.2.327–39); the representatives of the Venetian state (Lodovico, Montano, Graziano and Cassio) who witness Iago's murder of his wife Emilia and Othello's suicide. The wicked Iago does *not* die and remains a lingering problem to the Venetian state at the end of *Othello*. He promises to remain silent forever, even when faced with torture:

IAGO
Demand me nothing. What you know, you know.
From this time forth I never will speak word.

(*Othello*, 5.2.309–10)

We know what we know because of what Shakespeare has shown us. He wants to let us into some, but by no means all, of his characters' minds. Shakespeare wants us to go on thinking about what we have heard Iago say beyond the scope of the play, keeping him alive and aggressively silent in order for us to do precisely that.

SHAKESPEARE THE POET

By far and away the most successful publications by Shakespeare in his lifetime were his two narrative poems, *Venus and Adonis* and *The Rape of Lucrece*.

The best-loved books get read to pieces, so much so, that only one copy of the first edition of *Venus and Adonis* (1593) survives (in the Bodleian Library, Oxford). Poems based on stories from Ovid started to become popular in Europe from the middle of the sixteenth century, and both of these works represent Shakespeare's own significant contributions to that literary vogue. For much of the poem the goddess of love is naked and begging for sex before Adonis, but he resists her advances. It is an erotic masterpiece, a tragi-comedy propelled forward by male sexual fantasy. Unsurprisingly, the poem was popular among university undergraduates. In 1600, the writer and Cambridge academic, Gabriel Harvey, observed that 'the younger sort take much delight in Shakespeare's *Venus and Adonis*.' Gullio, a character in one of the three *Parnassus* plays, student entertainments about college life performed at around the same date by Cambridge students, says that he will honour 'sweet Master Shakespeare' and that to do so he will sleep with a copy of *Venus and Adonis* under his pillow.

Shakespeare produced his two narrative poems in 1593 and 1594 when the theatres were closed for almost two years because of the plague. Both poems include fascinating physical descriptions of bodies and facial expressions, as if Shakespeare were directing his own theatre of the mind. The descriptions provide insight into the kind of theatre that Shakespeare himself most wanted to see, and was used to seeing from the actors he worked with. You can almost imagine the following as Shakespeare's own advice to his players. From *Venus and Adonis*: 'I'd like you to "stop [...] his lips / And, kissing, speak [...], with lustful language broken"' (lines 46–7); 'When he breathes on you, could you "feed [...] on the stream as on a prey" (line 63)?'; and 'Could you deliver the line more as though you had "fear lurk[ing] in [your] eye", please (line 644)?'. From *The Rape of Lucrece*: 'Could you mix sighs with the little you have to say (line 563), "which to [your] oratory [would] add [...] more grace" (line 564)?'; 'Try putting "the period [or full-stop] often from [its] place, / And midst the sentence so [would your] accent break [...] / That twice [you would] begin ere once [you] speak [...]" (lines 565–7)?'; 'Could the on-stage crowd create such an impression that the audience "might see [your] far-off eyes look sad" (line 1386), and when you re-enter please could you march "on with trembling paces" (line 1391)? Thanks.'

Lucrece (1594), which Shakespeare himself called 'a graver labour' in his dedicatory epistle for *Venus and Adonis*, is resolutely tragic in tone. It too is erotic, but darkly so. Any sexual arousal that it inspires will implicate the reader in King Tarquin's raping of Lucrece (which leads – eventually – to her suicide, as well as to the end of the Roman monarchy). Although the act of rape itself is not described (though it seems to take place at some point between lines 680 and 686), the reader is drawn into something with which he or she should not want to be complicit. The claustrophobic moment during which Tarquin looks at Lucrece and gains his necessary erection is one of the most physically erotic passages in all of Shakespeare. Notice how, in the second stanza quoted here, the consistent lengthening of the rhyme royal lines with the unstressed syllable '-ing' seems to imitate Tarquin's throbbing tumescence:

> So o'er this sleeping soul doth Tarquin stay,
> His rage of lust by gazing qualified,
> Slaked not suppressed for standing by her side.
>> His eye which late this mutiny restrains
>> Unto a greater uproar tempts his veins,
>
> And they like straggling slaves for pillage fighting,
> Obdurate vassals fell exploits effecting,
> In bloody death and ravishment delighting,

Nor children's tears nor mothers' groans respecting,
Swell in their pride, the onset still expecting.
   Anon his beating heart, alarum striking,
   Gives the hot charge, and bids them do their liking.

His drumming heart cheers up his burning eye,
His eye commands the leading to his hand.
His hand, as proud of such a dignity,
Smoking with pride marched on to make his stand,
On her bare breast, the heart of all her land,
   Whose ranks of blue veins as his hand did scale
   Left their round turrets destitute and pale.

(The Rape of Lucrece, lines 423–41)*

'Proud' often referred to male sexual arousal, as did 'stand', so 'standing by her side', 'proud of such a dignity', 'pride marched on to make his stand' are all part of this vivid description of one of the most infamously aggressive erections anywhere in literature. 'Proud of this pride' and 'to stand in thy affairs' are the terms used to describe the poet's own erection in Sonnet 151. But in *Lucrece* the sexuality is presented through the terrible parallel violence of pillaging and the suffering of innocent mothers and children. Shakespeare at once draws the reader in with a complicit eroticism and supplies the opportunity for the reader to feel self-disgust.

'SUGARED SONNETS'

Shakespeare's Sonnets continue to inspire complicated reactions as well. It has too often been assumed that those published in 1609 represent a coherent sequence that tells the story of Shakespeare's life. Many readers find it impossible to disassociate the first person of the Sonnets, the 'I', from Shakespeare himself. The matter is complex. The 'I' both is and is not Shakespeare some or all of the time; art both is and is not autobiographical.

A dominant and still popular reading strategy (since the late eighteenth century) has been to try to identify real-life protagonists in the Sonnets – 'the young man', 'the dark lady' and 'the rival poet' – and then to find people in Shakespeare's life who might take those roles. But this is a limited, simplistic and short-sighted way of approaching some of the greatest, most varied and nuanced poems in the English language. In fact only twenty of them are unambiguously addressed to a male subject (real or imagined) and only seven of them definitely concern a female subject, but even these poems need not be addressed to the same male and female subjects. The remaining one hundred and twenty-seven Sonnets might be addressed to either a male or a female – that is, they have a universal application – or they are abstract and addressed to no one (for example Sonnets 94, 116 and 146). Even though Sonnet 144 mentions two loves, one of 'comfort' ('a man right fair'), and one of 'despair' ('a woman coloured ill'), that does not mean that only those two lovers (real or imagined) should be applied biographically to all one hundred and fifty-four poems, but this is what most critics have done for around two hundred and fifty years. Instead, we ought to be able to imagine as many different addressees as there are sonnets for them, since the terms of address within them vary.

Close analyses of their language and style suggest that the Sonnets were not written in the order in which they are printed which contradicts any notion that they represent an intended sequence. Rather, they are an anthology. In 1598, the clergyman and scholar, Francis Meres, referred to Shakespeare's 'sugared sonnets among his private friends' in his book *Palladis Tamia: Wit's Treasury*. Either Meres himself was one of Shakespeare's 'private friends', or he had caught sight or heard of some sonnets by Shakespeare being passed around literary London. The Sonnets were not published until a decade later and may or may not include the poems to which Meres refers. In any case, Shakespeare could have been revising his poems at any point up until their appearance in 1609.

Far more life-giving than any biographical reading is to accept Shakespeare's Sonnets as poems written on diverse occasions, some to or for real people (like Sonnet 128 perhaps), others as poetical essays (such as Sonnet 116). Some of them might well include personal confessions (perhaps Sonnet 36); others might be sketches for speeches that Shakespeare never augmented or set into a fully dramatic context.

It is worth bearing in mind, too, that there are other sonnets embedded within the plays throughout the whole of Shakespeare's career. *Romeo and Juliet* is structured around the sonnet form. It begins with a sonnet, a sonnet introduces act two, the lovers speak a shared sonnet when they first meet (1.5.92–105), and the tragedy ends with a truncated sonnet. Helen writes a letter to the Countess in the form of a sonnet (*All's Well That Ends Well*, 3.4.4–17); Jupiter speaks an extended sonnet to Posthumus (*Cymbeline*, 5.5.187–207) and the Epilogue to *All is True* (*Henry VIII*) is a sonnet in rhyming couplets. That the sonnet form was a vehicle through which Shakespeare cast imaginary thought and feeling again raises questions over the prevalent biographical approaches to these remarkable poems.

Two other poems are worthy of special mention. The book called *Shakespeare's Sonnets* 'never before imprinted' also contains a 329-line poem, 'A Lover's Complaint'. 'Complaints', or laments, were popular in the late sixteenth century and were sometimes printed at the end of sonnet sequences. 'A Lover's Complaint' is a deliberately enigmatic poem which never makes clear who the 'Lover' of the title is: the young maid, the young man, or perhaps the lonely, first-person narrator (who might be male or female), lying down on a hillside and hearing this 'plaintful story from a sist'ring vale.' (line 2). The poem echoes the themes, moods and ideas that run through the preceding sonnets and can be read as Shakespeare's own creative reflection on his collection.[20]

And no reading of Shakespeare as a poet is complete without trying to engage with his most mysterious and unusual work of all, a 67-line poem which has come to be known as 'The Phoenix and Turtle' (the 'Turtle' is a turtledove). This was Shakespeare's response to a commission, along with other leading poets, from Sir John Salusbury upon his knighthood. It was published in *Love's Martyr: or Rosalind's Complaint* by Robert Chester (1601) and printed, like the narrative poems, by Richard Field of Stratford-upon-Avon. 'The Phoenix and Turtle' is at once hauntingly medieval and challengingly metaphysical. Ostensibly about two birds, mourned by a whole company of birds, the poem gradually unfolds a description of love both real and lost:

> So between them love did shine
> That the turtle saw his right
> Flaming in the Phoenix' sight.
> Either was the other's mine.

('The Phoenix and Turtle', lines 33–6)

The poem is a tragedy in miniature and ends with a short funeral rite. The Phoenix and the Turtle, enigmatically 'enclosed in cinders', demand as much pity as do Romeo and Juliet or Antony and Cleopatra: 'for these dead birds sigh a prayer' (line 67). Shakespeare's (unusually female) Phoenix does not rise from the ash at the end, except in the mind of the reader who knows that that is what phoenixes do. Perhaps this is Shakespeare's own subtle way of igniting something of his own muse of fire within us, one deeply significant example of how he continues to empower us throughout the whole body of this work.

4

THE POWER OF SHAKESPEARE

Shakespeare's language inspires actors to portray a heightened reality, which in turn invites the audience to accompany them on a powerful emotional journey. We know whenever we arrive at a theatre to watch a Shakespeare play that, for the better part of three hours, something significant is about to unfold; so much so that it is often said that Shakespeare shows us what it is to be human. This chapter sets out to illustrate the power of his *making* as a dramatic poet – his depiction of thought and emotion – by considering six topics: love; war; history; mortality; transgression; and forgiveness.

MAKING LOVE

Romeo and Juliet speaks to anyone who has dared to love across a divide. The play's romance is set against the violence on Verona's streets between two feuding families, the Capulets and the Montagues. Juliet Capulet and Romeo Montague have fallen in love at first sight at the Capulets' masked ball (which Romeo and his friends have gatecrashed in disguise). Their famous 'balcony scene' takes place on a knife's edge: 'If they do see thee, they will murder thee', says Juliet (2.1.112). Their eloquence when speaking together for around 150 lines is wrapped up in the romance of daring and escape, 'I have night's cloak to hide me from their eyes', says Romeo (2.1.117). We listen as they find a way of speaking that we have not heard in the play until this point. Although their dialogue resonates with references to Elizabethan culture and mentions falconry, schoolboys and their books, and merchandise from the new world, a sense of timelessness is achieved because the lovers see themselves in the context of eternity. Juliet says:

> My bounty is as boundless as the sea,
> My love as deep. The more I give to thee
> The more I have, for both are infinite.

(2.1.175–7)

The scene is made powerful by its impassioned lyricism. When Romeo hears Juliet repeating his name and then calling back at him we hear:

> It is my soul that calls upon my name.
> How silver-sweet sound lovers' tongues by night,
> Like softest music to attending ears.

(2.1.209–11)

The language, rich with sibilant sounds, is close to music. In performance, Shakespeare's dramatic truthfulness is often best served through honouring the musicality to be found in his language. The best Shakespearian actors do not shy away from near-aria moments such as these, while at the same time making them sound sincere. These three lines illustrate how Shakespeare often universalises personal emotion. Romeo's 'soul' (Juliet) calls out his 'name' and leads him into a meditation of two lines about the musicality of all 'lovers' tongues' (voices) being like music in the night.

Romeo and Juliet depicts a tough-edged sexuality. Shakespeare changes Juliet's age from the source story, making her only thirteen (the same age as his own daughter, Susanna, at the time he wrote the play). While she is waiting for Romeo on their wedding night, Juliet speaks an excited soliloquy. She longs for the coming of 'gentle', 'loving, black-browed

night' so that she and her new husband, Romeo, can consummate their secret marriage and enjoy sex:

> Give me my Romeo, and when I shall die
> Take him and cut him out in little stars.

(*Romeo and Juliet*, 3.2.21–2)

'Die' was slang for the experience of orgasm, and perhaps Shakespeare's imagery here is his way of describing what orgasm feels like: it is to be cut up into 'little stars' and to experience a moment of infinity.

Queen Cleopatra of Egypt wants to die because her lover Antony has killed himself out of love for her, as well as shame of himself. As she prepares for her suicide she recalls their lovemaking:

> His delights
> Were dolphin-like; they showed his back above
> The element they lived in.

(*Antony and Cleopatra*, 5.2.87–9)

One interpretation of her abiding memories is that she is recalling the movement of his back and buttocks, moving and leaping like a dolphin as he thrusts into her. A few moments later, just before she allows the poisonous asp to bite her, she says 'Husband, I come' (5.2.282). As Juliet called for the coming on of night, so Cleopatra calls for the coming of her husband, the darkness of death, and sex, all at the same time; then, as now, 'come' meant to experience orgasm. Cleopatra well understands that

> The stroke of death is as a lover's pinch,
> Which hurts and is desired.

(5.2.291–2)

The tragedy of *Antony and Cleopatra* and *Romeo and Juliet* is what Richard Wagner called the Liebestod, the love-death narrative. The lovers have no choice but to take their lovemaking and their sexual experience to their graves, even though we know they would give everything for just one more night together.

Shakespeare delights in comic lovemaking, too. One of the most abiding of all stage-pictures is surely Titania, the Queen of the Fairies, making love to the simple, homely Nick Bottom who has had a spell cast on him to give him a donkey's head in *A Midsummer Night's Dream*. Shakespeare combines sentiment, humour and lyricism with sex:

> Come, wait upon him, lead him to my bower.
> The moon, methinks, looks with a wat'ry eye,
> And when she weeps, weeps every little flower,
> Lamenting some enforcèd chastity.
> Tie up my love's tongue; bring him silently.

(3.1.189–93)

These lines end the scene and in some productions lead to a great procession as the attendant fairies lead Bottom off the stage to the place of sex. When we next see this unlikely couple, performance often presents Bottom as exhausted with lovemaking while Titania is ready for more, Shakespeare's own stage version of Botticelli's great painting *Venus and Mars*: 'O how I love thee, how I dote on thee!'

says the Queen of the Fairies as her donkey-man falls asleep in her arms (4.1.44).

As You Like It is the play that contains the most marriages at the end: Touchstone and Audrey, Silvius and Phoebe, Celia and Oliver, and Rosalind and Orlando. The god of marriage himself, Hymen, appears on stage finally to bring about these pairings. But it is the journey towards these marriages rather than the marriages themselves that the audience is asked to enjoy. The main focus of our attention is watching the hero, Orlando, fall in love with another young man Ganymede (his beloved Rosalind in disguise). In the presence of Rosalind's cousin Celia, they even enact a betrothal rite known as hand-fasting (4.2.107–37). The moment is the closest Shakespeare comes to portraying what we now call a gay marriage. When Rosalind finally becomes Orlando's wife he, she and we all know that he is so deeply in love with her person that it matters not a jot whether she is male or

TITANIA

BOTTOM

female. While disguised, she has been able to see his undefended heart open to the possibility of a homosexual love. She has seen him fall for another man, who happens to be herself.

Same-sex love ripples through the canon: Antonio for Bassanio in *The Merchant of Venice*, Antonio for Sebastian and Duke Orsino for his pageboy (Viola in disguise) in *Twelfth Night, or What You Will*, and Achilles for Patroclus, who enjoy sex in their tent while the Trojan war rages around them, in *Troilus and Cressida*. The two noble kinsmen, Palamon and Arcite, see themselves as:

> one another's wife, ever begetting
> New births of love; we are father, friends, acquaintance;
> We are in one another families.

> (*The Two Noble Kinsmen*, 2.2.80–83)

Palamon asks: 'Is there record of any two that loved / Better than we do, Arcite?' (2.2.112–13). A few seconds later, their masculine love will turn to rivalry for Queen Hippolyta's sister, Emilia, whom they see from their prison window. One interpretation might see her entrance as ruining everything. A couple of scenes earlier we have heard Emilia herself describe her own female-female love for Flavina (who has died). She recalls the plucking of twin flowers and the placing of them between Flavina's breasts. Emilia concludes:

> That the true love 'tween maid and maid may be
> More than sex dividual [than between the separate sexes].

> (*The Two Noble Kinsmen*, 1.3.81–2)

She goes on to say that she will never love a man (1.3.86). Her feelings and perspective change when the noble kinsmen Palamon and Arcite start to war for her affections.

Shakespeare's Sonnets have come to represent love in its rich variety, too. Within them we find some of the finest and most memorable articulations of love's many moodedness in the English language. Among the Sonnets we find an intensity of romance and commitment: 'So long as men can breathe or eyes can see / So long lives this, and this gives life to thee' (Sonnet 18); there is mourning for lost love: 'weep afresh love's long-since-cancelled woe' (Sonnet 30); there is a longing for love: 'All days are nights to see till I see thee' (Sonnet 43); there is cynicism about love: 'So true a fool is love' (Sonnet 57); there is love-sickness: 'my love was my decay' (Sonnet 80); love brings youthfulness: 'love is a babe' (Sonnet 115); and there is a philosophical sense of absolutism in love: 'Love's not time's fool' (Sonnet 116).

Sonnet 130 is worthy of particular notice since in it Shakespeare playfully subverts and parodies the Petrarchan convention of love, which had been (and still was) dominant in love poetry across Europe for the better part of three centuries. In Petrarchan love, the woman was always the unattainable ideal for whom the man pined, like Romeo's for Rosaline before he meets Juliet (1.2.199–235). Not so for Shakespeare in Sonnet 130 in which the physical reality of the mistress contradicts a series of romantic clichés. It opens with the declaration that 'My mistress' eyes are nothing like the sun' and goes on to tell us that coral is redder than her lips, her breasts are a dull brown colour rather than snow-white, there are no roses in her cheeks, no perfume in her breath, no musical tone in her voice. No goddess she. The simple rhythm, the metrical feet of Shakespeare's own verse, is good enough for someone who defies all false comparison. There is a sudden change of tone in the couplet as the poet sets his mistress apart from all convention and celebrates her beauty, which is beyond all comparison:

> I grant I never saw a goddess go:
> My mistress when she walks treads on the ground.
> And yet, by heaven, I think my love as rare
> As any she belied with false compare.

> (Sonnet 130, lines 11–14)

Shakespeare's loving, in its many forms, always has its feet on the ground, which can rejoice in love's earthiness, its honesty and full sexual expression, as much as in its potential to transcend death.

MAKING WAR

England at war with itself or internationally forms some or all of the main plot for almost a third of the plays, including the three parts of *Henry VI*, the two parts of *Henry IV*, *Henry V*, *King John*, *King Lear*, *Macbeth* and *Cymbeline*. The Roman plays *Julius Caesar* and *Coriolanus* include civil rebellion and war. *Troilus and Cressida* depicts the tiredness and bitterness of the Trojan War (comparable to the weariness and ongoing expense of England fighting Spain in the Netherlands during Shakespeare's own time). Three other plays have soldiers as their leading characters: Titus

Andronicus has fought ten years for Rome and lost twenty-one of his sons in battle; Othello defends the Venetian Empire against the Turkish fleet near Cyprus; Macbeth fights valiantly for Scotland against the invading Norwegians. In three other plays, war forms a prominent part of the background. *Much Ado About Nothing* begins with the Prince of Aragon and his comrades returning from battle only to turn into a 'merry war' between the flirtatiously argumentative lovers Beatrice and Benedick (*Much Ado About Nothing*, 1.1.59); Prince Fortinbras is seeking to revenge his father and leads a successful Norwegian invasion on Denmark in *Hamlet*; and in *All's Well That Ends Well*, Bertram escapes to the Italian wars rather than stay with his wife Helen, whom he has been forced to marry.

Although war figures prominently in his plays, Shakespeare clearly deplores it. Any glorification of warfare is intermittent, brief and always self-questioning. While the seduction of performance can make it thrilling to see Caius Martius enter, covered in blood, during the Battle of Corioles (*Coriolanus*, 1.9), and while his heroism wins him the name Coriolanus, his politics become repulsive to the people of Rome. Of all the plays, *Henry V* is the most focused on war, its preparations, what it means to those involved and its lasting effects. The church is clearly shown to be implicated in what amounts to an illegal invasion of a foreign country. The Archbishop of Canterbury's long speech outlining Henry V's claim to the French throne is confusing, deliberately dull, and should raise a laugh or two when performed (*Henry V*, 1.33–95). With this speech, Shakespeare is satirising the entire basis of Henry V's invasion of France, which constitutes the whole story of the play.

In the Chorus's opening lines to Act Two we hear the euphoria that the beginning of war often brings:

> Now all the youth of England are on fire,
> And silken dalliance in the wardrobe lies;
> Now thrive the armourers, and honour's thought
> Reigns solely in the breast of every man.

> *(Henry V, 2.0.1–4)*

Yes, the play has its great stirring speeches, such as Henry V's clarion cry –

> Once more unto the breach, dear friends, once more,
> Or close the wall up with our English dead.

> *(Henry V, 3.1.1–2)*

– but even that thirty-four-lined speech (which ends with the King imploring his men to cry 'God for Harry, England and Saint George') is immediately undercut with the start of the next scene. Bardolph, Nym, Pistol and an anonymous young boy are lagging behind. The 'breach', or the front line, is understandably the last place they want to be. 'Would I were in an alehouse in London', says the Boy, 'I would give all my fame for a pot of ale and safety' (*Henry V*, 3.2.12–13).

Later, on the night before the decisive Battle of Agincourt, Shakespeare puts into the mouth of the English soldier, Michael Williams, one of his most direct anti-war speeches. He, along with his comrades John Bates and Alexander Court, is talking with the king who is in disguise and moving among his troops to help boost their morale. Williams starts to imagine war's effect on the king's own conscience:

> But if the cause be not good, the King himself hath a heavy reckoning to make, when all those legs and arms and heads chopped off in a battle shall join together at the latter day, and cry all, 'We died at such a place' – some swearing, some crying for a surgeon, some upon their wives left poor behind them, some upon the debts they owe, some upon their children rawly left. I am afeard there are few die well that die in battle, for how can they charitably dispose of anything, when blood is their argument?

> (4.1.133–42)

This conversation touches the King deeply, and when his soldiers leave him he speaks two soliloquies about the burden of war on the King's own conscience (4.1.227–81 and 286–301). In these speeches he envies his subjects' ability to sleep after a day of honest work while he bargains and prays with the 'God of battles'. King Henry V does indeed achieve victory the next day, despite his army being hopelessly out-numbered by the French, but Shakespeare takes pains to show that he is no war hero: Henry V orders the murder of all the French prisoners, an implicit act of brutality which contravenes the codes of combat (4.6.35–9).

Shakespeare details the effects of the war on the French landscape and its people with the Duke of Burgundy's eloquent and poetic speech, which repays close attention. Its poetry makes present the beauty of the natural world, which has now vanished as a result of the ravages of war and consequent neglect:

> And all our vineyards, fallows, meads, and hedges,
> Defective in their natures, grow to wildness.

> (5.2.54–5)

In his treatment of war, Shakespeare has a lot in common with Wilfred Owen, the brilliant and too-young-dead poet of the First World War. Like Owen, Shakespeare sees war's devastation and futility. *Henry V* ends with a sonnet which looks forward to the bloody Wars of the Roses during the reign of the weak Henry VI, 'whose state so many had the managing / That they lost France and made his England bleed.' (*Henry V*, Epilogue, lines 11–12). It is in *Henry VI Part Three* that the King himself watches and overhears a son who has unknowingly killed his father and a father who has unknowingly killed his son during the civil war. King Henry VI is overtaken with grief:

> Woe above woe! Grief more than common grief!
> O that my death would stay these ruthful deeds!
> O, pity, pity, gentle heaven, pity!

> (*Henry VI Part Three*, 2.5.94–6)

For Shakespeare, as for Wilfred Owen, it is the pity of war that in part provides the poetry. Both poets dare to tell the truth to cultures for which war felt essential, if never really glorious.

MAKING HISTORY

As well as setting out to dramatise key events during the reigns of English monarchs, Shakespeare is deeply interested in making ordinary people an extraordinary part of his history plays. The two parts of *Henry IV*, as much as they are about court life and the civil rebellion against Henry (who deposed the rightful king Richard II), have much to do with the garrulous, apparently irrelevant world of the Eastcheap tavern, The Boar's Head. The pub was a place of legend, where 'wild Prince Harry', the Prince of Wales, enjoyed getting drunk before taking up his royal responsibilities. These two history plays are very much about the personal formation of Prince Harry into King Henry V.

But there is a deeper, apparently non-historical interest at work. In the *Henry IV* plays Shakespeare brings on to stage the larger than life Sir John Falstaff. He embodies a dramatic life force of a kind that the English stage had never before seen. The key to understanding (and indeed performing) Falstaff is to recognise that he lives in an eternal present moment of pleasure. We miss the point entirely if we start to judge him morally. He lives for alcohol, comfort, other people's attention and sex. He is ever so fat, delights in excess and exaggeration, and is himself the constant butt of Shakespeare's incorrigible humour. Falstaff is a comic magnet, but is given moments of great pathos, too. In short, he becomes a living embodiment about why Shakespeare is writing history: Falstaff inhabits a world of the ordinary, which he makes extraordinary. History, in the *Henry IV* plays, is to be found in the here and now in which we too can find something of ourselves.

In *Henry IV Part Two*, the Lord Chief Justice challenges Falstaff about his 'great infamy', the robbery of pilgrims on Gad's Hill, his association with Prince Harry, his age and personality. Falstaff replies that he 'was born about three of the clock with a white head and something a round belly.' (*Henry IV Part Two*, 1.2.187–89). He is self-consciously timeless, born already an old man in the middle of the afternoon. His presence always signifies escape, roguishness and the importance of sheer exuberance. Falstaff's friends, lovers and sparring partners Mistress Quickly (whose name suggests a 'quick-lay') and Doll Tearsheet (whose name suggests a bed sheet torn in sexual excitement as well as one stained with tears) adore him, love him and hate him. In performance, their reactions to Falstaff being called away to likely military action (though not if he can help it) can be moving:

> DOLL TEARSHEET [*weeping*] I cannot speak. If my heart be not ready to burst – well, sweet Jack, have a care of thyself.
> SIR JOHN Farewell, farewell!
> *Exit [with Bardolph, Peto, and the Page]*
> MISTRESS QUICKLY Well, fare thee well. I have known thee these twenty-nine years come peascod-time, but an honester and truer-hearted man – well, fare thee well.
>
> (*Henry IV Part Two*, 2.4.382–8)

There is ample scope for laughter in that exchange, too, especially if Falstaff exits with self-conscious heroism and if, by the end of her speech, Mistress Quickly realises perhaps that the man she loves has not really been all that honest and not very true-hearted.

When Shakespeare is making history he is in part evoking the story of people passed over in the writing of the history books. Falstaff, his companions and counterparts (Bardolph, Nym, Peto, Poins, Mistress Quickly and Doll Tearsheet, and the aged Justices of the Peace Robert Shallow and his Cousin Silence) collectively take up much of the stage time in the two parts of *Henry IV*. Their dialogue is written entirely in prose, which allows them to occupy a dramatic texture of warm sentiment and humour as well as one of relaxed and unbuttoned reflectiveness. They are totally irrelevant to the story of King Henry IV, but they are everything when it comes to Shakespeare's helping us to experience history. It is as if he is dramatising the feeling of remembering where we were when significant historical events took place. The poet T. S. Eliot describes history as 'a pattern / Of timeless moments' and goes on to say that 'History is now and England' ('Little Gidding' in *The Four Quartets*). Shakespeare is dramatising that same kind of poetic reality.

MAKING MORTALITY

There are many times when Shakespeare invites us to share a defiant life force in the face of hopeless odds. Claudio, condemned to death for getting Juliet pregnant outside wedlock in *Measure for Measure*, articulates a fear of death and the unknown:

> Ay, but to die, and go we know not where;
> To lie in cold obstruction, and to rot;
> This sensible warm motion to become
> A kneaded clod, and the dilated spirit
> To bathe in fiery floods…

(Measure for Measure, 3.1.118–22)

His language is powerful because of the use of monosyllables in that first line, a favourite device of Shakespeare to catch our attention and refresh our listening. He combines, too, a Latinate vocabulary – 'obstruction', 'sensible', 'motion', 'dilated' – with a simpler, Anglo-Saxon one: 'cold', 'rot', 'clod', 'floods', 'bathe' and 'fiery'. The language yokes together the four elements of earth ('clod'), air ('spirit'), water ('bathe') and fire ('fiery'). That Claudio imagines bathing in 'floods' of fire combines two of these opposing elements to convey his inner sense of fear. Later in the play, the condemned Barnardine is awoken elsewhere in the prison and told that the day of his execution has finally come. He is drunk, hung-over and defiantly refuses to die:

> BARNARDINE I swear I will not die today, for any man's persuasion.
> DUKE But hear you—
> BARNARDINE Not a word. If you have anything to say to me, come to my ward, for thence will not I today.

(Measure for Measure, 4.3.56–60)

Although Barnardine's sentence of death has not been lifted, his protest, as far as we know, works, and his life, albeit on death row, continues. His obstinacy makes him no less than a life force, and one that resonates significantly in a story which dramatises the effects of denying life, exuberance and sexuality.

There are moments, too, when characters let go of an old way of life and step bravely into a new one. In *All's Well That Ends Well*, the cowardly Captain Paroles, who has been tricked by his friends and fellow soldiers into betraying them under the pain of torture and death, is left ashamed, friendless and broken. But he manages still to find hope in life:

> Captain I'll be no more,
> But I will eat and drink and sleep as soft
> As captain shall. Simply the thing I am
> Shall make me live [...]
> There's place and means for every man alive.

(*All's Well That Ends Well*, 4.3.332–5, 340)

A similar example, but one tragically focused on death, comes with Hamlet's readiness to die as he approaches the fateful duel with Laertes:

> Not a whit. We defy
> augury. There's special
> providence in the fall of

BARNARDINE

a sparrow. If it be now, 'tis not to come. If it be not to come, it will be now. If it be not now, yet it will come. The readiness is all. Since no man has aught of what he leaves, what is't to leave betimes? Let be.

(*Hamlet*, 5.2.165–70)

Hamlet's invocation of the gospel about a God who holds in love even the humble sparrow (Matthew 10:29) leads him to accept his own destiny. The prose is all-encompassing, carefully shaped and is followed (in the second quarto version only) by the simple, understated 'Let be'. This acceptance of life *and* death is perhaps Shakespeare's finest articulation of what it means to be a tragic hero, a human being caught up in the inevitability of a tragedy.

MAKING TRANSGRESSION

Shakespeare is fascinated by the criminal mind as well as by the effects of criminal action on the perpetrator. Richard III murders his way to the crown and is haunted in his dreams by the eleven ghosts of his victims on the night before his own death at the Battle of Bosworth. Although he then has a twenty-nine-line, justly famous soliloquy, shot through with self-questioning, it is his understated confession to Sir Richard Ratcliffe a moment later that conveys volumes about the King's emotional state: 'Ratcliffe, I fear, I fear' (5.5.168).

Macbeth also murders his way to the crown and Shakespeare achieves powerful effects through the language that portrays his inner feelings. Actors are often perceived as failing in the role of Macbeth. One reason is that the power of the poetry is so intense that an audience needs longer to digest it than is possible during a live performance. Impressive imagery flashes before us. When, towards the end of Act One, Macbeth almost convinces himself that he should not murder King Duncan he imagines the effect of the crime like this:

> His virtues
> Will plead like angels, trumpet-tongued against
> The deep damnation of his taking off,
> And pity, like a naked new-born babe,
> Striding the blast, or heaven's cherubin, horsed
> Upon the sightless couriers of the air,
> Shall blow the horrid deed in every eye
> That tears shall drown the wind.

(Macbeth, 1.7.18–25)

King Duncan's many good qualities will blow like angels on heavenly trumpets in protest. Pity itself will be born anew and the angels themselves will ride on the currents of the air like horses, showing the murder to the whole world and prompting sufficient tears to overwhelm the entire element of air. This is Shakespeare at his most vividly surreal and visually extravagant. So impressed was William Blake (1757–1827) with Shakespeare's imagery at this moment that he painted it as 'Pity' (c.1795).

A similarly bizarre image occurs a few moments later in the following scene. Macbeth is on his way to kill King Duncan and pauses to see the famous imaginary, air-born dagger ('Is this a dagger which I see before me?' 2.1.33), and to notice the personification of Murder leading the way to the scene of the crime, like the rapist Tarquin in *Lucrece* (*Macbeth*, 2.1.52–6). As soon as he has murdered King Duncan, Macbeth's transgression turns into tormenting guilt. He begins to feel that he has murdered sleep as well. He will never rest properly again and his wife, too, will be haunted with sleepwalking nightmares because of her part in the murder (*Macbeth*, 5.1.). So terrible is the King's blood

MACBETH

on Macbeth's hands that he imagines being able to turn the whole of the world's ocean into blood:

> Will all great Neptune's ocean wash this blood
> Clean from my hand? No, this my hand will rather
> The multitudinous seas incarnadine
> Making the green one red.

(Macbeth 2.2.57–61)

To convey the horror of Macbeth's realisation, Shakespeare invents a new verb, 'to incarnadine', that is to turn into the colour of raw flesh. In a King Midas-like way, Macbeth now imagines that if he were to touch the ocean it would turn every sea in the world into the colour of blood. That is how guilty he feels (and there is also a submerged allusion to the first plague of Egypt, when the God of Israel, through Moses, turned the River Nile into blood, Exodus 7:20).

Macbeth's transgression evokes the infamous King Tarquin, who raped Lucrece. Giacomo in *Cymbeline* thinks about Tarquin, too (2.2.12–14). He has tricked Princess Innogen into looking after his travelling trunk in her bed-chamber. When she falls asleep, the lid opens, and sometimes in performance Giacomo clutches the side of it, vampire-like, before he sits up. The scene can definitely be nightmarish and generate nervous laughter: there really *is* somebody lurking in that Ottoman trunk at the end of your bed. He speaks forty lines during which he commits to memory an inventory of her bedroom in order to prove he has been there and to win a wager he has made with her husband that he can violate Innogen's chastity. We are asked to imagine a silence so profound that we can hear the singing of crickets. There is an atmosphere of claustrophobia during which Giacomo makes extraordinarily detailed observations of Innogen's naked body and slips her bracelet from her arm. His act of transgression is made electrifying because Innogen might awake at any moment. The whole episode is dark and brooding and amounts to a visual rape:

> On her left breast
> A mole, cinque-spotted, like the crimson drops
> I'th'bottom of a cowslip.

(Cymbeline, 2.2.37–9)

Suddenly and surreally, Shakespeare takes us into a country meadow to look closely at the inside of a wild flower, even at the point at which the villain Giacomo is gazing and grazing most intently on his victim. Innogen remains asleep. It was midnight (2.2.2), but by the end of the speech, we hear the clock strike three; Giacomo has been visually raping Innogen for three hours. His transgression makes him feel as though he is in eternal damnation: 'hell is here' (2.2.50). Although he has not committed *actual* rape in the legal sense, he has proved himself to be a *virtual* Tarquin in deed. But unlike Tarquin, Giacomo has not been able to satisfy the reality of his lust. Instead, he climbs back into the trunk – burning with unfulfilled desire – and shuts the lid.

All of these acts of transgression illustrate major points of conflict and tension in Shakespeare's dramaturgy. He wants to make the danger and awfulness of the situations as real as possible by opening up the imaginary, criminal mind to us.

MAKING FORGIVENESS

Shakespeare is a great writer about forgiveness. As much as he dramatises forgiveness, there are characters who refuse it, as well as those who are unable to give it. Malvolio seems set never to forgive those who have gulled him. His final line is the haunting, bitter and pathetic 'I'll be revenged on the whole pack of you' (*Twelfth Night, or What you Will,* 5.1.374). *The Tempest* can be read as being all about the magician Prospero's calling together a reunion of the Neapolitan court in order to forgive them for usurping him twelve years earlier. But Antonio, who took the Dukedom from him (and who earlier says 'I feel not / This deity in my bosom' 2.1.282–3), remains stonily silent in the face of being forgiven (5.1.132–6), a silence that achieves its maximum effect only in live performance.

Forgiveness (which should be not be confused with either 'pardon' or 'mercy') shines most impressively in *The Winter's Tale.* This late play encompasses destructive jealousy, the betrayal of friendship, attempted murder, the intervention of divine justice, the death of a young prince and his mother the Queen, a bear coming onto the stage to chase away and eat a courtier (*'Exit, pursued by a bear'* 3.3.57), a pastoral world in which we see a new love recreated, and the reunion of a royal family. And Time. Sixteen years pass between the end of act three and the beginning of act four, when the personification of Time itself appears on stage to tell us what has been happening. All the actors who appear in both parts of the play must look and behave sixteen years older in acts four and five. *The Winter's Tale,* as its title suggests, is partly about how human beings survive coldness and suffering and arrive at the coming of spring and new life.

But Queen Hermione is not really dead. She only appeared to have died of shock on hearing about the death of her son, Prince Mamillius (3.2.141–52). For sixteen years her husband, King Leontes, whose jealousy led to his condemning her, has been in mourning, racked with guilt. Believing their new daughter to be begotten by his friend, King Polixenes, Leontes had the baby sent away sixteen years ago. Hermione has been hidden and looked after by Paulina. In act five, the lost Princess Perdita returns to meet the father she has never known, along with her husband-to-be, Prince Florizel (the son of Polixenes).

In the final moments, Paulina presents a statue of the dead Queen to King Leontes, King Polixenes, Princess Perdita, Prince Florizel, their courtiers and friends. Everyone is captivated with the artistry of the statue and astonished at how lifelike it appears. Paulina says she can make it move:

PAULINA It is required
You do awake your faith. Then all stand still.
Or those that think it is unlawful business
I am about, let them depart.
LEONTES   Proceed.
No foot shall stir.
PAULINA   Music; awake her; strike!
Music
(*To Hermione*) 'Tis time. Descend. Be stone no more.
Approach.

Strike all that look upon with marvel. Come,
I'll fill your grave up. Stir. Nay, come away.
Bequeath to death your numbness, for from him
Dear life redeems you.

(*The Winter's Tale*, 5.2.94–103)

And then the statue comes to life. Our 'faith' that Paulina has asked us to awake is answered. In the context of the story, the moment and the music that we hear are truly magical. If we did not know the play, the coming to life of the statue would be as great a miracle for us as for the characters watching it on stage. Shakespeare's *coup de théâtre* achieves its impact partly through the actress playing Hermione having to remain totally still for around 85 lines (about five minutes of stage time). This physical challenge seems almost unachievable by any actor, and yet this is what Shakespeare demands. Paulina's words, 'I'll fill your grave up. Stir. Nay, come away' convey a profound strangeness.

Husband and wife are reunited after sixteen years. Leontes reaches out to Hermione in amazement and says 'O, she's warm!' (5.2.109). The touch he has longed for is given back to him and the first thing he notices is the shock of her flesh and blood reality. The emotions of both husband and wife are too powerful for Shakespeare to put into words. Instead, we hear the observations of two onlookers – 'She embraces him', 'She hangs about his neck' – as Shakespeare dramatises what it means for two human beings to start to experience forgiveness. And then a daughter, who was supposed dead, is given back to her mother, who blesses her, Hermione's only words in the scene. Husband and wife may still have a lot of talking to do, but a possibility of reconciliation and mutual forgiveness has been opened up, and the effect on the audience can be deeply moving.

I well recall Gregory Doran's 1998 production for The Royal Shakespeare Company. As the actors came on to the stage for their curtain call, a woman sitting next to me turned to me with tears in her eyes and said, 'She was alive for sixteen years and nobody knew.' A little while later, as the theatre was emptying, I saw a friend and Shakespeare scholar staggering up the aisle with tears in his eyes, too. He grabbed my arm and said: 'You can keep your *Hamlets*, you can keep your *Othellos*; give me *The Winter's Tale* any day.' For many people, it is genuinely the most moving of all of Shakespeare's works.

It is worth noting that in Shakespeare's source story the Leontes figure, Pandosto, kills himself and no reunion or forgiveness occurs. Although Shakespeare's emotional and artistic visions are entirely different, forgiveness comes at a cost. Prince Mamillius and the courtier Antigonus (who was eaten by the bear) remain dead. Leontes's mention of 'this wide gap of time' in the play's penultimate line acknowledges the pain as well as the love that he has caused and experienced. But he *is* forgiven. And that is the wonder of this wintry play.

* * *

Attempting to convey the power of Shakespeare is an endless task. He is never afraid to address the worst and the best of human experiences and to ask the big questions.

When King Lear carries on to the stage his dead daughter Cordelia he asks:

> Why should a dog, a horse, a rat have life,
> And thou no breath at all?

(The Tragedy of King Lear, 5.3.282–3)

The vocabulary Shakespeare uses in moments of extreme emotion is often straightforward, and sometimes, as here, entirely monosyllabic. By this point in a production we have witnessed Lear's suffering for over three hours. That we should now arrive at this apparently simple articulation makes it one of the most powerful questions about the nature of human existence ever asked.

To hold a copy of Shakespeare's *Complete Works* is to have an apparently endless illustration of the joys and pains of human life, our brightest and darkest imaginings. Our reading, however powerful, is always open to change, challenge and surprise by the ways we may encounter Shakespeare in performance.

5

ENCOUNTERING SHAKESPEARE

When performed live Shakespeare's work of art erupts before us. We are struck by many lively and immediate components: music, song, plays within plays, pageants and processions, duels (and, in *As You Like It*, a wrestling match), armies, battles, swords and suits of armour, stage blood, gunshots, severed heads, corpses littering the stage (a headless one in *Cymbeline*), crowds pressing against each other in ancient Rome, the silent observers in a scene, how the actors move, the mood that they bring on or take off the stage with them, the effect of their voices, facial movements and gestures, the visual seduction of costumes and lighting, and staging effects (many of which are quite extreme, for example, Titus Andronicus cutting off his own hand and Gloucester's eyes being gouged out in *King Lear*). We hear laughter, sometimes in unexpected places, and become sensitive to the reactions of other audience members.

We should ask ourselves whether the text has been abridged, expanded or manipulated in ways that affect interpretation. Are there any cross-gendered casting choices or meaningful doublings of roles, such as Cordelia and the Fool in *King Lear*, or Theseus and Oberon in *A Midsummer Night's Dream*? What age are the characters being played and what difference does this make (for example, an older

Beatrice and Benedick or Romeo and Juliet)? The ways in which people are killed or wounded tell their own stories about their characterisation and relationships. Do any of the actors establish memorable connections with the audience, for example, by addressing one or more individuals directly, or even through physical contact? Is there an interval and how does this affect the tempo of the play? And, importantly, where is the play set? In a recognisable social world? Are we in the present or the past, and, if so, when and why? Or is the whole play set somewhere more abstract and absurd? Shakespeare can often thrive on having no heavily visual design and (perhaps ideally) can sometimes work best – especially outdoors – with no set at all.

All of these factors and possibilities are invisible to us until we attend a live performance. Together, they provide the beginnings of a checklist of things to look out for when we watch Shakespeare. It might be the first time we have seen a particular play, or it might be a play we already know well. Whatever knowledge or experience we have, it is worth reminding ourselves that each production is its own adaptation of the text. Shakespeare's words in whatever edition we read them are only the starting point for a director and company of actors to produce a new work of art in its own right: the production itself. The more theatre we see, the more productions of the same play we can weigh against each other, the more critically aware we become.

Are, for instance, all the characters we expect to see actually present in a production? If I were to see a production of *Hamlet* that cut the character of the Norwegian Prince Fortinbras (a choice made by Laurence Olivier for his influential 1948 film version) it would be immediately clear that the director had chosen to emphasise a particular narrative trajectory which has excluded important aspects of how Shakespeare told the story. There might be practical reasons for doing without Fortinbras. *Hamlet*, which can sometimes be around four hours long, becomes much shorter. But to lose Fortinbras is also to make the story introverted; without him the play can only be about the Danish royal family and their attendant neuroses. 'Something is rotten in the state of Denmark' (1.4.67) signals that *Hamlet*, a state-of-the-nation play, is a political drama, not only a familial one. The reason why the soldiers are on the battlements when the play starts is that they are keeping watch for a threatened Norwegian invasion. Like Hamlet and, later in the play, Laertes, Fortinbras is seeking revenge for his father: three dead fathers, three angry sons. No Fortinbras means that King Claudius needs no foreign policy. Without a Fortinbras there would be no need for Hamlet to speak the impressive soliloquy (from the second quarto version) that begins 'How all occasions do inform against me' (Additional Passages, 4.4.23). He has just seen Fortinbras arrive in Denmark (on his way to conquer Poland) and shares his wretched feelings about having been unable to achieve any revenge so far, takes stock of his situation, and meditates on the futility of armed combat. A production with no Fortinbras usually ends elegiacally with Horatio mourning his dead friend with the lines:

> Good night, sweet prince,
> And flights of angels sing thee to thy rest.

> (5.2.311–12)

But what of the alternative? Shakespeare wants us to see the young Prince Fortinbras enter. We have heard of him intermittently and seen him briefly. Now he comes to restore order, view the dead bodies, and take up the crown of Denmark for himself. A production at this point will look ahead to what his new monarchy might be like. Is he tyrannical? Does he remind us of any well-known political leader? Does he enter heroically, like a golden boy, who comes to rescue Denmark from corruption and decadence? He is there to bring new life to the state, but what will that mean to Denmark under Fortinbras? In one production I know of, the first thing Fortinbras did was to have Horatio taken out and shot, ensuring that there would be no one left to tell a competing historical narrative. As a dramatic presence in *Hamlet,* Fortinbras forces us to think politically. So whether he is present or not makes an enormous difference to the overall tone and story of the play. But that is a difference that can only strike us when we see the play performed.

At the same time, we should resist being tricked into thinking that we are ever having the play presented to us as Shakespeare himself intended it. The fact that the production before us, for example, might have been designed to be acted in Elizabethan or Jacobean costume makes it no more 'Shakespearian'. We are twenty-first-century people. A doublet and hose takes us no closer to Shakespeare's play or dramatic meaning than a pair of jeans and a T-shirt. The international theatre director Michael Bogdanov, who has devoted much of his career to Shakespeare, always insists that the plays are performed in modern dress. He believes that 'if, for one moment, and one moment only, a point of contact and identification is made in the present, then the play immediately becomes a play of our time. That is why Shakespeare has been called the greatest living dramatist, and *Hamlet* the enduring piece of *contemporary* theatre.'[21] Hamlet himself expresses similar sentiments about the players who arrive at Elsinore when he calls them 'the abstracts and brief chronicles of the time' (2.2.527–28) and says that the purpose of playing is 'to hold as 'twere the mirror up to nature, to show virtue her own feature, scorn her own image, and the very age and body of the time his form and pressure' (3.2.22–4).

The decision to stage Shakespeare in modern dress is one way for a production to invite the audience to think afresh. Theatre is a place for debate and a highly interpretative director who presents the play through his or her own political lens can often produce the most engaging Shakespeare. A production is not for all time, only for its own time. Those which set the play in the past, or in an undefined, generic version of the past, are every bit as political as modern-dress Shakespeare. The problem is that they can often feel as though they are not concerned with politics at all, which is precisely part of their political effect. If our encounter with Shakespeare on the stage is primarily about a pretty and romantic story in gorgeous costumes, we risk not being encouraged to think, and might leave the theatre having tasted little more than a sweet-tasting sedative. But whatever the period in which a production is set, what matters most is how well the story is told, whether we believe what the actors are saying, what it is we are invited to think about, why a particular production is taking place now, and why it is as it is. One of the greatest compliments that can be paid to a production is the comment I hear from time to time when leaving the theatre along the lines of, 'they must have modernised the language because I understood every word of that'. What this kind of appraisal indicates is that the actors have so understood and absorbed Shakespeare's language that they have been able to render it comprehensible to modern ears.

It is important to talk about the theatre productions we see because interaction and opinion are the lifeblood of the art form. Theatre is a sociable expression of culture, calling upon our responses, hoping to etch experiences in our individual and collective memories. In engaging with theatre history we might encounter different records of performance: photographs, programmes, an annotated script of the production on which the cuts and cues have been marked (the prompt book), and archive video and sound recordings. But it is through the theatre review that we often most vividly discover what a production was like, its performances, interpretative choices, and whether it was insightful or not. But reviews will only ever be as good as the person who writes them, and that is a large and subjectively inflected variable.

None of us can see all the productions that might take our fancy, so I usually want a review to be descriptive about what particular actors did, or to describe any significant cultural or political responses. Usually, the most helpful reviews are produced by writers who know the play well and have seen other productions of it. Engaging with a plurality of responses to the same production often yields insights that would be missed if we read only the opinions of a select few, or our own favourite theatre critic.

It matters what we say about the productions we see, but it matters most that we actually do talk about what we see or,

better still, produce our own record of the event. Some people have found the following questions helpful as a way of reflecting on the Shakespeare we see in performance:

- How did the production make you feel?
- What is worth remembering about this production?
- How does this production speak to our own times?
- Why is *your* opinion valuable?
- Was there a moment that encapsulated this production for you?
- What difference would you like your review to make?[22]

If we go to see our next Shakespeare production bearing these questions in mind, then we will probably have a lot to talk about afterwards. But however we approach theatre reviewing, we need to take a deep breath and be brave. The cost of our ticket, a company's reputation, and what we hear other people saying might distract us from forming our own opinion, but we owe it to each other to speak honestly about the Shakespeare we encounter in the theatre. Quite often, the most enjoyable productions are to be found on the amateur scene or by low-budget professional companies whose need to produce a particular play is undeniable and can be palpably felt. But wherever and however we encounter Shakespeare, as far as theatre reviewing and talking about productions are concerned, honesty is always the best policy. One of the final lines of *King Lear* provides the best touchstone or mantra I know for theatre criticism: 'speak what we feel, not what we ought to say.'

In performance it can sometimes take only an apparently

incidental moment, one phrase even, to make all the difference to our understanding. The novelist Margaret Drabble had the good fortune to go to school with Judi Dench whom she remembers playing Ariel in *The Tempest*:

> Nearly sixty years later I can hear her voice, as Ariel describes the pitiable state of the bewitched and shipwrecked king and his followers, and assures her master Prospero that if he were to see them now he would pity them: 'if you now beheld them, your affections / Would become tender' (5.1.20–21). Prospero responds, 'Dost thou think so spirit?' (5.1.22) – to which she replies, 'Mine would, sir, were I human' (5.1.22–3). Judi Dench uttered that phrase, 'were I human', with such unearthly yearning that whole vistas of depth beyond depth in the meaning of the play opened before us. Such moments of revelation a truly fine performance can offer. They are worth as much as many pages of critical analysis. And Judi was only seventeen.[23]

Such can be the rewards of theatre-going, great acting and excellent writing. Encountering Shakespeare in performance can turn the plays we think we know inside out and reveal unsuspected treasures just below the surface. And it is always in the hope of such treasure that I go back to see the same plays time and again.

SPEAKING SHAKESPEARE

One way of encountering live Shakespeare without having to go to the theatre is to read it aloud. The Sonnets are a good place to start. Reading a single sonnet aloud well will take us close to Shakespeare's language and lyricism. What we learn in miniature when speaking a sonnet, we can then apply to his larger body of work. Sonnets are often a favourite focus among voice coaches and directors working with actors.

What do you need to be mindful of before you start reading a Shakespeare sonnet? Well, for one thing, you don't need to be able to act in order to render a good reading, since speaking a sonnet is not the same as performing it. Performance assumes a sense of characterisation and an emotional reality. Reading a sonnet is more about being hypersensitive to the language, image and, importantly, the sonnet's sound.

It is a good idea to read a sonnet three times through before starting to converse with yourself or anyone else about it. Try whispering it first of all. This will immediately lift the words off the silent page and start to release their music. When we read a sonnet aloud, it is good to recall and to try to convey something of the sonnet's initial intimacy. I once heard the actor Jeffrey Dench (brother of Judi Dench) remark that 'however large the audience, a sonnet when read has always got to sound like pillow talk.' We will almost certainly encounter difficulty on our first reading – a hard to understand image, phrase or word. But our first read-through might register the length of its lines, the sound of the rhymes, whether there are any repetitions, the shape of the sonnet, its conceit, and a sense of its journey. Try whispering Sonnet 73:

That time of year thou mayst in me behold
When yellow leaves, or none, or few, do hang
Upon those boughs which shake against the cold,
Bare ruined choirs, where late the sweet birds sang.
In me thou seest the twilight of such day
As after sunset fadeth in the west,
Which by and by black night doth take away,
Death's second self, that seals up all in rest.
In me thou seest the glowing of such fire,
That on the ashes of his youth doth lie,
As the death-bed whereon it must expire,
Consumed with that which it was nourished by.
   This thou perceiv'st, which makes thy love more strong,
   To love that well, which thou must leave ere long.

TRY WHISPERING IT FIRST

THEN AT CONVERSATIONAL VOLUME

Now read it a second time at your usual, conversational volume. This should reveal more of what the sonnet requires us to visualise. In Sonnet 73, we are presented with 'yellow leaves', 'boughs which shake against the cold', 'twilight', the fading sunset, and 'black night'. There are also a glowing fire, a 'death-bed' and ashes. We might notice any irregular line endings, or enjambments (when the sense flows over onto the next line, as in lines 2–3) that might make a special demand on where we can take a breath. And we might be struck by some of the vowel sounds, the internal word-music. There is a supreme example of this in Sonnet 73: 'Bare ruined choirs, where late the sweet birds sang'. The long, open vowels of this single line make it sound as though it were exploring the full range of notes available.

A third reading might notice the value of each of the three quatrains (the three lots of four lines up to line 12) and a sense of who is involved in the poem. Is there an intimate 'thou' or a more formal 'you'? How does the speaker, the imaginary 'I' of the poem, position him or herself in relation to the addressee, and what might this convey about the personalities involved? After a third reading, the overall meaning, tone and effect of the sonnet may well be making itself palpably felt to us.

What should we pay attention to in trying to speak a sonnet well? Here are six things to bear in mind.

First, use your own voice. Do not try to put on a poetic or Shakespearian voice, or a particular kind of accent. Shakespeare comes most vividly to life when we speak his words in the voice we would use to talk to our friends because it will resonate authentically. But as Touchstone says in *As You Like It*, 'the truest poetry is the most feigning' (3.3.16–17) and the important difference between speaking Shakespeare and ordinary conversation is that we need to honour the full value of his words, their vowel sounds (long or short, open or closed), the delight of the consonants that help shape the ends of words or that make them kick in the middle, and to look out for words which rhyme, and make them chime. In short, when we try to read a Shakespeare sonnet, we are seeking to make real a heightened and, in many cases, a lyrical language. The verbal music of Shakespeare is there for our taking and our sounding, if we are prepared to seize it and allow it to be heard.

Second, look out for antitheses. Technically, this simple rhetorical figure relates to conflict and opposition. When speaking Shakespeare we need to pay attention to how words are set against each other in the same line of verse. The speaker might notice a relationship of balance between the words. So, in Sonnet 73: 'That *time of year* thou mayst in me *behold*' (with emphasis on the particularity of a time and the beholding of its effect); 'When *yellow leaves*, or none, or few, do *hang*' (emphasising a sense of scarce survival); 'Upon those *boughs* which shake against the *cold*' (with the emphasis on the physical sensation of the tree exposed to autumn), and moving through the same sonnet we might notice the more genuinely antithetical setting of 'ruined choirs' (leafless trees, tattered pages of a book, or perhaps the deserted choir stalls of ruined abbeys) against 'sweet birds' (which can evoke 'choristers'), of 'twilight' against 'day', 'Death's' against 'rest' (sleep), 'ashes' against 'youth', 'consumed' against 'nourished', and so on. Word balance or antithesis is present in almost every line and can often be sounded and experienced through a slight pause in the middle of a line, for example, 'Which by and by [*imperceptible pause*] black night doth take away', or 'In me thou seest [*imperceptible pause*] the glowing of such fire.' This is what the great actress Edith Evans called 'poise', a tension that holds the words together and keeps us listening.

Third, pay attention to the personal pronouns. We could read this sonnet once through and exaggerate these in order to establish the pathways of relationship and conflict between the poet and the addressee and other subjects in the poem. A good reading never finally exaggerates the personal pronouns, or even draws too much attention to them, but knowing that they are emphatically there will help them to resonate as important emotional and dramatic presences.

Fourth, it is useful to be aware of the ends of the lines, to point them up a little. Try to resist running each line into the next line, even when there is no punctuation to hold you back. Line endings help to distinguish verse from prose. They are there to help the reader and aid the meaning. The word 'hang' at the end of line 2 can be squeezed, wrung a little, momentarily sounding the suggestion of melancholy in 'none, or few' yellow leaves. If 'hang' is allowed to hang (with a short pause after it), then the pay-off comes with the rhyming 'sang' two lines later. Similarly, 'fire' at the end of line 9 is ignited by 'glowing' just before it: 'fire' might then achieve something of an erotic charge in the voice. The word can be held on the breath, the vowel sound keeps the mouth open, but only briefly. Consider the words at the ends of the lines as almost like dotted crotchets in music. They are worth their time, and half again. In a Shakespeare sonnet the last word of each line will always pay you extra if you observe and honour its full value.

Fifth, recognise the architecture of the sonnet, often three quatrains and a couplet, with a volta (a turning point) at line 9 or at line 13. In Sonnet 73 the three quatrains present a series of developing images. The couplet is the turning point, as well as the climax. Each quatrain can be treated as a little story in its own right. To approach a sonnet like this will mean that the reader does not give away all of his or her gifts at once.

Sixth, do not be tempted to 'perform' the sonnet, as to do so would be to push too hard on it. Shakespeare's Sonnets can take whatever you bring to them, but 'acting' a sonnet risks obscuring, if not squashing, possible nuance and a sense of multidirectional meaning. To read a sonnet well requires work, dedication and sensitivity. They are at once delicate and direct and need to be treated gently. It is no good shouting at them or over-insisting.

Speaking a sonnet, like reading any Shakespeare aloud, requires practice based on close reading and listening. It is about experiencing the poetry much more intimately than is usually possible in a theatre. The good news is that Shakespeare's sonnets require plenty of digestion. One at a time is plenty. If you are new to them, you might like to dip into the collection and read any that takes your fancy, since they do not need to be read in the order they are printed. Or, after having tried Sonnet 73, you might like to start by working your way through the following: 12, 17, 18, 27, 29, 30, 71, 98, 129, 130, 138.

So, you might like to try reading the sonnet three times through then having some fresh air – open a window, step outside or go for a short walk. Then read the sonnet again and go through the six directions outlined above. After some more fresh air, perhaps repeating some of the phrases you most like over and over to yourself, you will have started to make the sonnet your own. Editions of the Sonnets can be pocket- or handbag-size and individual poems, copied out onto a small piece of paper, can fit into a wallet or a purse. You might read the sonnet you are practising to yourself when you are out on your next walk.

As a rule of thumb, a Shakespeare sonnet should take no more than a minute

REPEATING THE MOST MEMORABLE PHRASES

ARCHITECTURE

TRY GOING FOR A SHORT WALK BETWEEN READINGS

PROGRESSION

to read (any longer and you might be being a bit self-indul-gent). Reading a sonnet well and then sharing it with a friend is perhaps one of the most intense ways of encoun-tering the power and the joys of Shakespeare's poetry and it will make you more sensitive to the ways in which his language is spoken by actors the next time you encounter him in the theatre. The power of Shakespeare's language is, after all, often one of the main reasons people give when they are trying to account for his greatness. Certainly it is one reason, but how else might we begin to respond to the question, 'Why Shakespeare?'

6
WHY SHAKESPEARE?

The Poet Laureate, Carol Ann Duffy, was only half joking when she said that for all writers, a visit to Shakespeare's Birthplace is like going to Bethlehem. Charles Dickens, whose novels are saturated with Shakespearian allusions, helped to raise money for the Birthplace in its early years, preferring it, rather than a statue, to be the lasting memorial. 'I find I take so much more interest in his plays, after having been to that dear little dull house he was born in!' says Mrs Wititterly in chapter twenty-seven of Dickens's *Nicholas Nickleby,* 'I don't know how it is, but after you've seen the place and written your name in the little book, somehow or other you seem to be inspired; it kindles up quite a fire within one.' The poet John Keats was certainly inspired by the genius of the place during his visit on 2 October 1817. In the Birthplace visitors' book, under 'Place of Abode', Keats wrote 'Everywhere'. When visiting Shakespeare's grave later that same day he expressed the same sentiment in the church's visitors' book, but in Latin, *'ubique'*. 'Everywhere' and

'Shakespeare' were clearly intimately connected in his mind. Keats, whose responses to Shakespeare are truly life-enhancing, will himself play a prominent part in what is to follow. His two signatures and the single words next to them serve as touchstones for the ways in which four centuries of readers, audiences, theatre practitioners, creative writers, political activists and critics have responded to the big question, 'Why Shakespeare?' Their answers are part of an ongoing tradition which might be called 'the Shakespeare effect', which often feels like it is 'everywhere' in our culture. Shakespeare '*ubique*': why?

RETELLINGS FOR CHILDREN

OPERA

MENDELSSOHN

TCHAIKOVSKY

MUSIC

WAYS IN

One way is to read the plays and poems but there are many other possibilities through which we might gain a sense of what Shakespeare is in our culture, from retellings for children to opera; from pieces of music and musicals to paintings and ballets; from advertisements to novels and poems; from political speeches to compulsory school assessments; from stage productions to news reports about political crises. These 'ways in' do not all lead to precisely the same place, but they all point in the same direction. 'Shakespeare' is a large, multifaceted, and polyphonic conversation.

Quite often one hears the story of an epiphany when, for somebody seeing Shakespeare performed live, everything seemed suddenly to make sense. Performances can be powerfully seductive and Shakespeare was writing, in the main, to be performed. 'I was thunderstruck', writes the novelist Jane Smiley on recalling a production of *Hamlet* when she was in twelfth grade, 'the play seemed to coalesce right before my eyes; the play belonged to me somehow.'[24] Many people who sympathise with her reaction will feel, as she did, that they own Shakespeare through understanding and enjoying a production of one of his plays. Certainly Smiley's account resonates powerfully with my own experience.

But there's also a long tradition of reading Shakespeare, being captivated by his words on the page. One of the most vivid accounts of reading Shakespeare is by the great eighteenth-century actress, Sarah Siddons, when she was preparing to play Lady Macbeth for the first time, a role for which she became famous:

> I went on with tolerable composure in the silence of the night (a night I can never forget), till I came to the assassination scene, when the horrors of the scene rose to a degree that made it impossible for me to get farther. I snatched up my candle, and hurried out of the room, in a paroxysm of terror.[25]

That is what reading Shakespeare late at night can do to you.

Another Shakespearian reader, with different ramifications, is Henry Crawford in Jane Austen's novel *Mansfield Park* (1814):

> Shakespeare one gets acquainted with without knowing how. It is a part of an Englishman's constitution. His thoughts and beauties are so spread abroad that one touches them

everywhere; one is intimate with him by instinct. No man of any brain can open at a good part of one of his plays without falling into the flow of his meaning immediately.

(*Mansfield Park*, chapter 34)

By the turn of the nineteenth century, Shakespeare's fate to be *everywhere* was sealed. Although Austen is clear about Henry Crawford's own enthusiasm for acting and performance, it is his reading Shakespeare aloud that prompts his sudden eulogy. He praises Shakespeare's articulacy and his 'beauties', possibly a reference to a hugely popular and influential eighteenth-century anthology by William Dodd *The Beauties of Shakespeare* (first published in 1752 and in its thirty-ninth version as late as 1893). Dodd's anthology bears out the long and popular practice of disseminating Shakespeare through his 'Greatest Hits'. Henry Crawford's approach, like that of many other readers, combines aesthetic judgement – Shakespeare's eloquence and his 'flow of meaning' – with his unchallenged popularity, his unquestioned 'beauties', or great moments. But Austen takes us into a political arena with Crawford's mention of 'an Englishman's constitution'. Perhaps writing with characteristically subtle irony Austen was being mindful of the fact that England has no written constitution, only a crown, or perhaps, in the end, only Shakespeare.

Shakespeare's popularity by the time Austen was writing *Mansfield Park* was a result of the rise of popular Shakespearian celebrations. People celebrate Shakespeare because they love him; they want to make him their own. Today, Shakespeare's birthday is celebrated all over the world in various ways, with special attention usually paid to important anniversary years. Celebration of this kind started in the eighteenth century. Peter Scheemaker's statue of Shakespeare was installed in Westminster Abbey's Poets' Corner in 1741 and 1769 saw the actor David Garrick's Stratford Jubilee. His special celebration marked the first time that Shakespeare broke out on to the streets among the people, free from the mediation of scholars, librarians or theatres. Garrick was invited by the Town Council of Stratford-upon-Avon to host a special Shakespearian pageant and more than exceeded their expectations. It began with the firing of canons at dawn and the young men of the town serenading the young ladies beneath their bedroom windows. A temporary theatre was built, but the proposed procession of Shakespearian characters was rained off, and the Avon flooded. A special rainbow-coloured ribbon was made for people to wear, representing Shakespeare's inclusivity of all political parties as well as the spectrum of his genius. There was horse racing and country dancing and a fancy-dress ball (to which the writer James Boswell went dressed as a Corsican chief, a political act of solidarity for the island seeking to maintain its independence against the invading French). Not a word of Shakespeare was spoken throughout the whole of the celebrations. But Garrick, wearing a medallion made from the mulberry tree supposed to have been planted by Shakespeare, spoke his influential Shakespeare Ode, some of which was set to music by Thomas Arne, the composer of 'Rule Britannia'. Garrick's Stratford Jubilee (which transferred as a successful show in its own right to London) succeeded in popularising Shakespeare for the age, and confirmed for the Kingdom of Great Britain (established by the union of Wales and England with Scotland in 1707) that Shakespeare was its national poet.

As British nationalism grew to become a dominant political force, Shakespeare was exported and adopted all over the world with the British Empire, along with the English language. Without the British Empire, Shakespeare would not enjoy the great sense of his being a single international currency. What is striking, though, is how Shakespeare remained behind, post-Empire, and became the favoured poet of many world cultures who have made him their own through translation, appropriation and adaptation. Shakespeare had become culturally promiscuous.

This is especially the case in America where, after the declaration of independence in 1776, Shakespeare started to become popular, a captivating immigrant who spoke to many different kinds of people. When two future presidents, Thomas Jefferson and John Quincy Adams, visited Shakespeare's Birthplace in 1786, Jefferson 'fell upon the ground and kissed it' while Adams chipped off a piece of wood from what he was told was Shakespeare's chair.²⁶ Writing about his nine-month journey across America in the 1830s, the young French aristocrat Alexis de Tocqueville, in his book *Democracy in America*, observed 'there is hardly a pioneer hut in which the odd volume of Shakespeare cannot be found. I remember reading the feudal drama *Henry V* for the first time in a log cabin'.²⁷ But Shakespeare has been – and perhaps still is – just as much a nationalistic cause in the States as anywhere else. It was in New York at the Astor Place Opera House on 10 May 1849 that severe rioting broke out because of objections that the British actor, William Charles Macready, was playing Macbeth against his rival, the American-born Edwin Forest, who was simultaneously performing in the role at the Broadway Theatre. Twenty-two people were killed amidst a mob of fifteen thousand.

Shakespeare has loomed large in politics ever since his own time. He himself had no choice but to live under an absolutist monarchy, a powerful head of state presiding over a parliament. But as the actor Ralph Fiennes says in light of having directed his own, politically edgy film version of *Coriolanus* (2011), 'Shakespeare is always questioning order, especially the right to rule'.[28] History proves that Shakespeare has often been used to speak to people living within oppressive regimes, whether that is in apartheid South Africa, where Janet Suzman's politically charged 1989 production of *Othello* at the Market Theatre in Johannesburg spoke powerfully to white and black audiences at a time when it seemed most needed, or Corinne Jaber's brave, 2005 Afghan production of *Love's Labour's Lost* in Kabul, which brought men and women together on stage for the first time in thirty years (and at a great personal cost to the actors who took part).[29] *Hamlet* became (and perhaps still is) the most relevant Shakespeare play for many of the former USSR Eastern-bloc countries, who found in it a parable about how the state can make inert the life of an individual. And Sonnet 66 has been translated many times to speak against political regimes in which 'art [is] made tongue-tied by authority' (line 9).

Shakespeare's political sensitivity can in part be traced through the history of international state censorship. By the middle of the nineteenth century, for example, Germany had effectively nominated Shakespeare one of its three national poets, along with Johann von Goethe and Friedrich Schiller, a cultural outcome of the deep affiliation the German philosophers, playwrights and poets had felt for Shakespeare from the beginnings of German Romanticism half a century earlier. The German Shakespeare Society, founded in 1864 (the tercentenary of his birth) is the oldest such association and the largest in Europe. Knowing the power of Shakespeare among the German people, Adolf Hitler's dictatorship banned productions of *Julius Caesar*. No tyrant would ever want to allow the staging of the pre-eminent play about the democratic assassination of a head of state. Many are the productions of *Julius Caesar* to have portrayed the eponymous character as Hitler, Mussolini, Franco, Castro or another dictator.

And it was *Julius Caesar* that the Shakespearian actor John Wilkes Booth had in mind when he assassinated President Abraham Lincoln on 14 April 1865. Another former President, Bill Clinton, writes:

> Abraham Lincoln, with access to so few books as a young man, did have access to Shakespeare, and the results speak for themselves.[30]

Clinton does not elaborate on which results he has in mind; Booth, however, had no doubts. In his mind, Lincoln was responsible for the oppressive war against the South and on the day he shot him, Booth wrote a letter by way of explanation, addressed 'to my countrymen'. He saw himself as a parallel to Shakespeare's own Brutus in *Julius Caesar*, 'I love peace more than life. Have loved the Union beyond expression', he writes, echoing Brutus saying to his countrymen: 'not that I loved Caesar less, but that I loved Rome more' (3.2.21–2). Booth's letter ends with him quoting Brutus:

> O, then that we [*sic.*] could come by Caesar's spirit,
> And not dismember Caesar! But, alas!
> Caesar must bleed for it!

(2.1.169–71)[31]

It is a chilling but undeniable parallel and acts as a sombre reminder of how often Shakespeare is invoked during times of extreme personal, political or national crises.

The ways that might lead us into Shakespeare include performance, reading, celebration, nationalism, political activism, rioting, revolution and even assassination. What all of these forces have in common is the shaping of the individual: Shakespeare becomes the most widely understood cultural testing ground in which we can better understand ourselves.

SHAKESPEARE AS A BLACK HOLE?

In the final chapter of his 1989 cultural history of Shakespeare from the Restoration to the present, the Shakespeare scholar and textual expert Gary Taylor argues that none of the defences of Shakespeare's 'singularity' ring true. But to my mind, to ask whether Shakespeare really is the greatest is to pose the wrong question, because to assume that he is means that you take on a position impossible to sustain.

There are many great writers, artists and musicians. Over the years, I have come not to believe in 'greatest' – but I do believe in greatness. Taylor ends his study by using the metaphor of Shakespeare being a 'black hole':

> His stellar energies have been trapped within the gravity of his own reputation. We find in Shakespeare only what we bring to him or what others have left behind; he gives us back our own values. […] His accreting disk will go on spinning, sucking, growing.[32]

Certainly, the kinds of cultural endeavours and reactions I have been describing illustrate the popularity and sheer inevitability of Shakespeare, Shakespeare by default, if you will. The conclusions Taylor comes to when thinking about Shakespeare as a 'black hole' are similar to the philosophical position adopted by Virginia Woolf who found within any work of art no intrinsic meaning but rather:

> that the whole world is a work of art; that we are parts of the work of art. *Hamlet* or a Beethoven quartet is the truth about this vast mass that we call the world. But there is no Shakespeare, there is no Beethoven; certainly and emphatically there is no God; we are the words; we are the music; we are the thing itself.[33]

Adopting Woolf's modernist or Taylor's postmodernist positions, or both, it seems that what we bring to Shakespeare is the greater part of what we find there. Or, as the Shakespeare critic Terence Hawkes has said, 'Shakespeare doesn't mean: *we* mean *by* Shakespeare'.[34] And, apparently, we can bring anything we like to the works. Shakespeare can and will take it, transform it, and hand it back to us, and hopefully our self-knowledge will be improved, and we will feel cleverer and more alive.

SHAKESPEARE AND I

Like many others I got started because of some inspirational schoolteachers.[35] My way in was through my comprehensive school, which means I am the product of a state educational system that, from the late 1980s, decided to make Shakespeare compulsory, and still does. As for most of my generation, therefore, I started relatively late, first properly engaging with Shakespeare at the age of fourteen when we studied *Macbeth*. I found within its language, its story, its performance (in the classroom, on audio recording and film, and in the theatre), its characters and their relationships, its dark imagination – which forces us to think about night, ravens, bloody daggers, murder, blood, tortured consciences, emotional and mental breakdowns, immense personal loss, trauma and a nation torn apart by war – a power so definite and undeniable, so all-embracing of my intellectual and theatrical interests and tastes, that Shakespeare quickly became the most challenging, disturbing and imaginative phenomenon that I had ever encountered. He wasn't easy. I do not believe he ever has been. But if something within his work can catch you (it might be a phrase, an image, a moment of performance) then Shakespeare can draw you in, and take you through such landscapes and soundscapes, such emotions, dramatic moments, and thoughts, that it becomes clear why he is fully deserving of his reputation.

Try these few lines from *Cymbeline*. Princess Innogen has said goodbye to her husband Posthumus, who has been banished. She does not know if she will ever see him again. Her servant Pisanio describes his parting and she responds:

> I would have broke mine eye-strings, cracked them, but
> To look upon him till the diminution
> Of space had pointed him sharp as my needle;
> Nay, followed him till he had melted from
> The smallness of a gnat to air, and then
> Have turned my eye and wept.

(Cymbeline, 1.3.17–22)

The imagery combines surrealism – the eye-strings stretching the eyeballs out of their sockets and the eye-strings themselves cracking under the strain – with an ordinary, domestic object, 'a needle', and a tiny insect, 'a gnat'. We are shown Posthumus becoming ever smaller on the horizon of Innogen's mind's eye. The lyricism of the verse along with its odd line-breaks evokes her out-of-breath emotion, and yet she remains controlled and poised. Had she been there, she says, she would have wept, but she wasn't. Keats again. The nineteenth-century Shakespeare scholar Charles Cowden Clark relates a story about Keats 'who as a schoolboy [...] was so moved by an image in *Cymbeline* of the departing Posthumus melting "from The smallness of a gnat to air" that his eyes, like Imogen's, filled with tears'.[36] Keats was responding with an emotional intelligence so finely tuned to Shakespeare that he himself was able to experience something of Innogen's own response. His reaction arose from how he read, but also because of the qualities of Shakespeare's writing and imagination.

His work can shock, amuse, move, comfort, inform, entertain, bore and appal. The novelist Leo Tolstoy is among those who have hated Shakespeare. His *Shakespeare and the Drama* (1903) criticised Shakespeare's characterisation for being unconvincing and attacked what he called 'the play of feeling', too much showy emotion. George Bernard Shaw, keen to introduce Tolstoy's work for its 1906 English translation, had a famous love-hate relationship with Shakespeare whom he criticised for his lack of moral philosophy, 'that his characters have no religion, no politics, no conscience, no hope, no convictions of any sort'.[37] But Shakespeare, unlike Shaw, never preaches. That difference between the two of them lies at the heart of Shaw's frustration. They are worlds apart as playwrights. I have never seen Shakespeare as a 'moral' writer; he does not show us how to behave or tell us *what* we should think. While some of his characters express moral views, he himself steps to one side, holds the situation at arm's length and allows us to think for ourselves. Shakespeare knows that there is no such thing as perfection, especially when it comes to family life. All families in Shakespeare are dysfunctional. He is never afraid to question, but, as the Shakespeare scholar A. D. Nuttall observes, 'Shakespeare would not be as impressive as he obviously is if he had done *nothing* but pose queries. He provides many answers, and sometimes these have more than a local efficacy. [...] Shakespeare, the supreme dramatist, is strong both on what would happen and what could happen.'[38]

If you think you are certain about your response to a

moment, then look again at who is speaking, who else is present on stage, ask yourself why these words are being spoken at this particular time, and the chances are that you will see the moment differently. And don't be tempted to think that any characters or moments are irrelevant. They all have their part to play in Shakespeare's overall design. Autolycus in *The Winter's Tale*, Pompey Bum in *Measure for Measure*, Trinculo in *The Tempest*, and Constable Dogberry in *Much Ado About Nothing*, for example, all emphasise, comment upon, relieve us from, or reveal to us something more about, the main action.

Shakespeare can stare life in the face, embrace pain and suffering as a fact, and then show us what life might be like if we hoped and imagined enough ('Prove true, imagination, O, prove true' as Viola says in *Twelfth Night, or What You Will*, 3.4.367). Or, he shows us what might happen if we were to behave too cruelly. The whole of *King Lear* seems like a warning about the collapse of civilisation. Human beings can all too soon become 'like monsters of the deep' and prey upon one another (*The History of King Lear*, 4.2.49). Shakespeare is open about human desires, whether they are sexual, political, religious, pioneering, ambitious, compassionate or controlling. He presents emotions that he never felt (the guilt after murdering a monarch, for example), and creates space for us to find something of ourselves in them, making them seem real. His words and ideas can shape our world. He provides us with all the material (sometimes too much) to judge for ourselves, and complicates any response that is at risk of being too straightforward. Keats (again!) wrote to his brothers George and Tom Keats in December

1817 about what he calls Shakespeare's 'negative capability, that is, when a man is capable of being in uncertainties, mysteries, doubts, without any irritable reaching after fact and reason'.[39]

Shakespeare is capable of letting characters express themselves directly. 'I do love nothing in the world so well as you. Is not that strange?' says Benedick to Beatrice in emphatic and simple monosyllables in *Much Ado About Nothing* (4.1.269–70).

> I never wished to see you sorry; now
> I trust I shall.

> (*The Winter's Tale*, 2.1.125–6)

says Hermione to her husband Leontes in *The Winter's Tale* when he falsely accuses her of adultery. 'Bear with my weakness. My old brain is troubled', says Prospero to Miranda and Ferdinand in *The Tempest* (4.1.159, what we sometimes call having a 'senior moment'). The effect in all of these examples is to disarm us, to provide us with a flash of insight, to make the moment and the speakers imaginatively real, just like one of us. 'Shakespeare knew', writes the poet and essayist Edith Sitwell, 'that there is no fragment of clay, however little worth, that is not entirely composed of inexplicable qualities'.[40] Sitwell reminds us to focus on Shakespeare's particularising qualities. He names characters we never see and makes them momentarily real, for example 'Marian Hacket, the fat alewife of Wincot' (*The Taming of the Shrew*, Induction 2, line 20); Alice Shortcake who borrowed the hapless Abraham Slender's Book of Riddles (*The Merry Wives of*

Windsor, 1.1.186–7); and 'little John Doit of Staffordshire, and black George Barnes and Francis Pickbone, and Will Squeal, a Cotswold man [...] and Samson Stockfish, a fruiterer' (*Henry IV Part Two*, 3.1.18–20, 31, and 39). Shakespeare is able to find poetic and dramatic energies as much in the minutiae of the everyday and in simple language as in great historical events, human crises or supernatural moments.

Shakespeare also presents us with moments of knotty difficulty, when his meaning becomes hard to understand and discern, even though the actual words themselves might not be:

> it is I
> That, lying by the violet in the sun,
> Do, as the carrion does, not as the flower,
> Corrupt with virtuous season.

(Measure for Measure, 2.2.170–73)

says Angelo in *Measure for Measure*. In *Troilus and Cressida*, Ulysses's densely worded speeches seem only to gesture towards clarity at first sight or hearing:

> And this neglection of degree it is
> That by a pace goes backward in a purpose
> It hath to climb. The general's disdained
> By him one step below; he, by the next;
> That next, by him beneath. So every step,
> Exampled by the first pace that is sick
> Of his superior, grows to an envious fever
> Of pale and bloodless emulation.

(Troilus and Cressida, 1.3.127–34)

Or Coriolanus's refusing to pity the people of Rome:

> That we have been familiar,
> Ingrate forgetfulness shall poison rather
> Than pity note how much.

(*Coriolanus*, 5.2.85–7)

Moments such as these (and there are many) require intellectual effort and concentration, and yield more to a close private reader than to a theatre audience who only hears them once.

The poet Gerard Manley Hopkins remarked, in a letter to his brother in 1885, that 'Shakespeare and all great dramatists have their maximum effect on stage but bear to be or must be studied at home before or after or both'. Shakespeare, he says, is best read as well as performed. It is not a case of either/or: Shakespeare is a thinker *and* a dramatist; he is a poet *and* a storyteller. We need to try to make our physical, mental and emotional energies available to these different demands if we are properly to engage with his work. We *become*, to some extent, *what* we engage with when we study, read or watch. 'Perhaps that is the great value of drama of the Shakespearian kind', writes poet W. H. Auden, 'that whatever [the spectator] may see taking place on stage, its final effect upon each spectator is a self-revelation'.[41]

So I arrive at my most honest and direct response to 'Why Shakespeare?': because we enjoy his work, and in the ways that mean most to us as individuals. The pursuit of Shakespeare – as of all great literature and art in general – is a justifiable hedonism. Enjoyment is the primary aim, and that enjoyment is justified because it develops within us a

deeper understanding of ourselves through a critical perspective. Or, as Keats concludes his sonnet 'On sitting down
to read *King Lear* once again':

> When through the old oak forest I am gone,
> Let me not wander in a barren dream,
> But when I am consumèd in the fire
> Give me new phoenix wings to fly at my desire.

'MACBETH' REVISITED

The poet Ted Hughes was deeply struck by the mythical
qualities in Shakespeare and found within the work an
overwhelming poetic vision:

> The actors and directors of his plays are fully aware of this.
> Immersed in the psychological realism of Lear, they know
> that the tiny, realistic remark "Pray you, undo this button",
> has to be placed at the centre of an event somehow as
> unearthly, awesome, wild, metaphysically grand as Blake's
> *Prophetic Books* and *The Book of Job* combined. They are
> aware that when Macbeth stalks out, drugged with his wife's
> domestic will, to kill King Duncan, it is a more momentous
> shifting of Heaven and Hell than when Satan lifts off in
> Milton's inferno. Everybody recognizes how all this gigantic
> accompaniment emerges from something other than realistic
> characterization.[42]

No wonder I was bowled over by *Macbeth* as a fourteen-
year-old. And perhaps Hughes's sense of Shakespeare's
deeply rooted life-force was what was being played out

when some years ago I was asked to organise a twenty-five-minute version of *Macbeth* for some pupils aged between six and ten at St Andrew's primary school in Shottery, near Stratford-upon-Avon.

The children had never seen live Shakespeare before, but had watched the Animated Tales version of *Macbeth*. 'At the moment', a member of staff told me, 'they think Shakespeare is a cartoon'. A friend applauded the project, 'Good idea. Introduce them to Shakespeare before anyone tells them that he's too difficult for them'. I cut just over four-fifths of the play and the staging was kept to a minimum. We performed it with eight people. Tomato ketchup was used for blood and the bowl of water which the Macbeths used 'to clear [them] of this deed' (2.1.65) between the extremely short scenes, doubled as the witches' cauldron. Macbeth and Macduff had simple, wooden swords for their final confrontation. During the performance, Macbeth's sword accidentally broke just before he died. A bloodstained bag containing a head-shaped something was held aloft at the end. The crown, which had changed heads twice, was placed on Malcolm.

At the end there were many interested questions from the children who seemed delighted with their first ever live Shakespearian encounter. It was as if the simple, dramatic process which they had just experienced was a kind of magic that they had to understand and explain. One asked 'What's in the bag?' They passed it around excitedly until someone guessed that it was a cabbage. There was a further gasp of revelation when I revealed a cauliflower. One boy asked whether the blood was real and one girl asked, quite vaguely but with her own conviction, 'How did you set it up?' The star of the show was, undoubtedly, the dagger, which was very real indeed and still sported some of Macbeth's blood when I allowed the children to look at it more closely. 'I've got a dagger at home like that' was one response. The final question was perhaps the most interesting of all. One boy simply asked, 'Is it true?' 'Do *you* think it's true?' I replied. 'Yes', he said. 'Then every word of it is true'. He smiled.

SO WHY SHAKESPEARE, AGAIN?

As those primary-school children recognised, Shakespeare tells a good story. He draws us in emotionally and intellectually. He makes us *feel* as much as he makes us want to answer, discuss and explain. At an unfathomable level those children were connecting with the mythical qualities of what they saw played out in front of them. The scholar Catherine Belsey has made a fascinating study of the fairy-tale and folk-tale elements in Shakespeare who, she says, knows:

> the power of a well-told tale to capture and hold the attention of an audience. Such narratives offer the best of recreation; at the same time, they come to inhabit our consciousness. In Shakespeare's case, if I am right, to a degree they are there already, and in the end perhaps that, above all, is why.[43]

Shakespeare's stories, his political and emotional realities, help to account for his translatability into other languages. Poetry is lost in translation, but can be re-invented.

Shakespeare in translation can often sound in the other language as brightly contemporary as a new playwright. Fresh translations are often commissioned for new productions of a play, and a modern idiom adopted. In English, our reading and performances are blessed by the poetry, but actors and audiences probably have to work harder to produce a relevant and life-giving meaning.

The World Shakespeare Festival in 2012, which formed part of the Cultural Olympiad, gathered and presented 73 productions in many different languages and cultures. Such a happening demonstrated, as Stanley Wells remarks, that 'both Shakespeare the artist and Shakespeare the catalyst, [is] a writer who, like Falstaff, is not only witty in himself but the cause that wit is in other men, a continuing source of pleasure but also a constant stimulus to critical thought, even to rebellion'.[44] Shakespeare has been used as a mouthpiece for the oppressor and his words are quoted during times of national and international crises. But more often he becomes a rallying point for the oppressed and disenfranchised. So the hugely influential African-American liberation poet and writer Maya Angelou (1928–2014), speaking in 1985 to the National Assembly of Local Arts agencies in Cedar Rapids, Iowa, could say of Shakespeare: 'Of course, he was a black woman. I understood that. Nobody else understood it, but I *know* Shakespeare was a black woman. That is the role of art in life'.

I KNOW SHAKESPEARE WAS A BLACK WOMAN. THAT IS THE ROLE OF ART IN LIFE.

MAYA ANGELOU

No one owns Shakespeare, though anyone can experience a sense of ownership of him. The genie escaped from the bottle with the publication of the Folio in 1623. Ever since then, Shakespeare has become a currency through which we can understand ourselves. If this does not make him the greatest of all artists, it certainly makes him among the most powerful, and I have yet to come across another artistic currency comparable to Shakespeare's. Performance; study; enjoyment; celebration; protest; rebellion; the telling of life-enhancing stories that have a mythical status; a literature which many cultures can appropriate and translate into their own; a black hole with the power to delight children in primary schools, and grown-up children for the rest of their lives: all this can Shakespeare truly deliver.

FURTHER READING

A good way of getting to know a play well is to read and dip into a variety of different editions of it. The Shakespearian's bookshelf is multicoloured, bearing as it does the spines of the best editions available across a range of critical series. After editions of plays come Shakespeare Studies more generally, and what follows is a highly selective list of recommendations.

Biographies

Jonathan Bate, *Soul of the Age: the Life, Mind and World of William Shakespeare* (2008): a thematically presented biography of Shakespeare's intellect.

Lois Potter, *The Life of William Shakespeare: A Critical Biography* (2012): especially strong on the theatrical context.

S. Schoenbaum, *William Shakespeare: A Documentary Life* (1975): an empirical corrective to return to often. A 'compact' version (just as useful) is readily available.

James Shapiro, *1599: A Year in the Life of Shakespeare* (2005): fresh and intensely contextual.

René Weis, *Shakespeare Revealed: A Biography* (2007): strong on the Stratford-upon-Avon background, daringly intimate and creative.

Theatre and Performance

John Barton, *Playing Shakespeare* (1984): actors discuss their approaches to Shakespeare (also a now classic television series available on DVD).

Michael Bogdanov, *Shakespeare: The Director's Cut* (2003): essays on the plays by a politically engaged, often controversial director.

Paul Prescott, *Reviewing Shakespeare: Journalism and Performance from the Eighteenth Century to the Present* (2013): what is theatre reviewing and how do we do it?

Edwin Wilson, ed., *Shaw on Shakespeare* (1961): an anthology of one of the funniest and liveliest of all Shakespeare critics.

Stanley Wells, ed., *Shakespeare in the Theatre: An Anthology of Criticism* (1997): a source book for some of the best and most useful writing about Shakespeare in performance from 1700 to 1996.

Players of Shakespeare (1988–2007), six volumes (editors include Philip Brockbank, Russell Jackson and Robert Smallwood): twelve essays in each by actors from The Royal Shakespeare Company.

www.reviewingshakespeare.com: a free online gathering of reviews of Shakespeare productions around the world made available by The Shakespeare Birthplace Trust, University of Warwick and Misfit, inc.

Criticism

Michael Dobson and Stanley Wells, eds, *The Oxford Companion to Shakespeare* (2001): an essential A–Z of Shakespeare Studies.

Margreta de Grazia and Stanley Wells, eds, *The New Cambridge Companion to Shakespeare* (2010): the latest iteration of a volume of essays about contemporary Shakespearian studies.

Ewan Fernie and Simon Palfrey, eds, *Shakespeare Now!* (from 2010): a series of fresh, experimental and original approaches.

Peter Holland, Lena Cowen Orlin and Stanley Wells, eds, *Oxford Shakespeare Topics* (from 2000): a series of distinguished introductions to different aspects of Shakespearian studies.

Stanley Wells, *Shakespeare: For All Time* (2002): an illustrated account of Shakespeare's life, artistry and impact on human creativity over four centuries.

Stanley Wells, *Shakespeare & Co.* (2006): a groundbreaking account of playwriting, collaboration and influence in Shakespeare's time.

For Children

The Usborne World of Shakespeare (2001): an illustrated historical and theatrical survey, with plot summaries and a who's who (8 years upwards).

The Usborne Illustrated Stories from Shakespeare (2010): six plays retold (for children who have just started to read alone).

Nick Walton and Christopher Lloyd, *The What on Earth? Wallbook of Shakespeare* (2014): the complete plays illustrated in an extraordinary fold-out format with a timeline (8 years and upwards).

NOTES

1. John Keats, *The Letters of John Keats*, ed. Robert Gittings (Oxford: Oxford University Press, 1970),
   p. 176.
2. This revisionist view is being led by David Fallow of the University of Exeter.
3. Jeanne Jones, *Family Life in Shakespeare's England: Stratford-upon-Avon 1570–1630* (Stroud: The Shakespeare Birthplace Trust, 1996), p. 90.
4. Andrew Gurr, *The Shakespeare Company 1594–1642* (Cambridge: Cambridge University Press, 2004), p. 89 and p. 108.
5. John H. Astington, *English Court Theatre: 1558–1642* (Cambridge: Cambridge University Press, 1999),
   p. 234 ff.
6. Gurr, *The Shakespeare Company*, p. 115.
7. Astington, *English Court Theatre*, pp. 234–50.
8. Mairi Macdonald, 'Not a Memorial to Shakespeare, but a Place for Divine Worship: The Vicars of Stratford-upon-Avon and the Shakespeare Phenomenon, 1616–1964', *Warwickshire History*, 11 (2001–2002), pp. 207–26 (p. 207).
9. Stanley Wells, *Shakespeare: For All Time* (Basingstoke: Pan Macmillan, 2002), pp. 98–9.
10. How Shakespeare's library has been differently imagined over the centuries is discussed in: Robert S. Miola, *Shakespeare's Reading*, Oxford Shakespeare Topics (Oxford: Oxford University Press, 2000), pp. 164–9.
11. Assonance: a repeated vowel sound. Onomatopoeia: the word sounds like the action or thing it is describing. Personification: describing a thing or concept as though it were a person. Adynaton: something that is impossible. Antithesis: one thing contrasts with another. Alliteration: words in a sequence that start with the same letter. Metaphor: connecting through similarities. Hyperbole: exaggeration. Repetition: speaking a word more than once. Synecdoche: a physical part represents the whole. Merism: referring to the constituent parts of something.
12. Levin's famous sentence begins: 'if you cannot understand my argument, and declare "It's Greek to me", you are quoting Shakespeare; if you claim to be more sinned against than sinning, you are quoting Shakespeare', etc. It is easily traceable online and was originally printed in: Bernard Levin, *Enthusiasms* (London: Coronet Books, 1983), pp. 167–8.

13. Hannibal Hamlin, *The Bible in Shakespeare* (Oxford: Oxford University Press, 2013), p. 234.
14. Christopher Marlowe, *The Complete Plays*, eds Frank Romany and Robert Lindsey (London: Penguin Books, 2003), p. 390.
15. Joy Leslie Gibson, *Squeaking Cleopatras: The Elizabethan Boy Player* (Stroud: Sutton Publishing, 2000), p. 66.
16. John Jowett, ed., *Sir Thomas More*, The Arden Shakespeare (London: A. & C. Black Publishers, 2011), p. 424.
17. Jowett, *Sir Thomas More*, p. 440 and p. 437.
18. The term was coined by Paul Edmondson and Stanley Wells, eds, *Shakespeare Beyond Doubt: Evidence, Argument, Controversy* (Cambridge: Cambridge University Press, 2013). See also our free e-book www.shakespearebitesback.com
19. William Shakespeare, *The Two Gentlemen of Verona*, eds Arthur Quiller-Couch and John Dover Wilson (Cambridge: Cambridge University Press, 1921), p. xiv.
20. Paul Edmondson and Stanley Wells, *Shakespeare's Sonnets* (Oxford: Oxford University Press, 2004), pp. 110–13.
21. Michael Bogdanov, *Shakespeare, The Director's Cut* (Edinburgh: Capercaillie Books Limited, 2003), p. 11.
22. See Paul Edmondson, Paul Prescott and Peter Smith, eds, *Reviewing Shakespearean Theatre: The State of the Art*, in the journal of The British Shakespeare Association, *Shakespeare* (2010), pp. 274–401 (p. 391).
23. Margaret Drabble, 'The Living Drama' in *Shakespeare and Me*, ed. Susannah Carson (London: Oneworld, 2013), pp. 412–17, p. 415.
24. Jane Smiley, 'Odd Man Out', in *Shakespeare and Me*, ed. Susannah Carson (London: One World Publications, 2014), pp. 407–11, p. 408.
25. Thomas Campbell, *Life of Mrs Siddons*, 2 vols (1834), vol. 2. pp. 35–36
26. James Shapiro, ed., *Shakespeare in America: An Anthology from the Revolution to Now* (New York: The Library of America, 2013), p. xxiv.
27. Alexis de Tocqueville, *Democracy in America*, trans. by Henry Reeves, rev. Francis Bowen, 2 vols (Cambridge: Sever and Francis, 1863), vol. 2, p. 66.
28. Ralph Fiennes, 'The Question of Coriolanus', in *Shakespeare and Me*, pp. 220–27, p. 225.
29. See Stephen Landrigan and Qais Akbar Omar, *Shakespeare in Kabul* (2012): an account of staging Shakespeare in Afghanistan for the first time (in 2005).
30. Bill Clinton, 'Foreword' to *Shakespeare in America*, p. xvii.
31. Shapiro, *Shakespeare in America*, p. 197.

32. Gary Taylor, *Re-inventing Shakespeare* (London: The Hogarth Press, 1989; repr. Vintage, 1991), p. 411.
33. Virginia Woolf, 'A Sketch of the Past' in: *Moments of Being*, ed. Jeanne Schulkind (London: Chatto and Windus for The University of Sussex Press, 1976), p. 72.
34. Terence Hawkes, *Meaning by Shakespeare* (London: Routledge, 1992), p. 3.
35. I want to add grateful acknowledgement to my teachers: Trish Ellison, Fiona Long and Jenny Wallace, who taught me English at Huntington School, York, from 1988–1992.
36. Jonathan Bate, *Shakespeare and the English Romantic Imagination* (Oxford: Clarendon Press, 1986), p. 157.
37. George Bernard Shaw, *Shaw on Shakespeare*, ed. Edwin Wilson (New York: Applause Books, 1961), p. 3.
38. A. D. Nuttall, *Shakespeare The Thinker* (New Haven and London: Yale University Press, 2007), p. 381.
39. John Keats, *The Letters of John Keats*, ed. by Robert Gittings (Oxford: Oxford University Press, 1970), p. 43.
40. Edith Sitwell, *A Notebook on William Shakespeare* (London: Macmillan & Co, Ltd, 1948), p. 1.
41. W. H. Auden, 'The Prince's Dog', in *The Dyer's Hand and Other Essays* (London: Faber and Faber, 1975; repr. 1987), pp. 182–208 (p. 182).
42. Ted Hughes, *Shakespeare and the Goddess of Complete Being* (London: Faber and Faber, 1992; repr. 1993), p. 37.
43. Catherine Belsey, *Why Shakespeare?* (Basingstoke: Palgrave Macmillan, 2007), p. 170.
44. Stanley Wells, 'Foreword' in *A Year of Shakespeare: Re-living the World Shakespeare Festival*, eds Paul Edmondson, Paul Prescott and Erin Sullivan (London: Bloomsbury, 2013).

ACKNOWLEDGEMENTS

My heartfelt gratitude is due to Paul Prescott and Stanley Wells for their careful reading of my work and for their honest comments and guidance. Their friendship and many kindnesses have been of immeasurable help in the writing of this book. I am grateful, too, to my editor, Michael Bhaskar formerly of Profile Books for all of his support and encouragement.

INDEX

IDEAS IN PROFILE
SMALL INTRODUCTIONS TO BIG TOPICS

Ideas in Profile is a landmark series of enhanced eBooks and beautifully illustrated print books that offer concise, clear and entertaining introductions to topics that matter.

Each enhanced eBook will have animated sequences illustrated by Andrew Park and **COGNI+IVE**, the team behind the renowned RSA Animates.

Visit www.ideasinprofile.com to watch the animations and find out more.

ALREADY PUBLISHED

Politics
by David Runciman

Art in History
by Martin Kemp

FORTHCOMING

Social Theory
by William Outhwaite

The Ancient World
by Jerry Toner

Criticism
by Catherine Belsey